Data Modeling for Quality

Delivering benefits through attention to detail

Graham Witt

Technics Publications

Published by:

2 Lindsley Road
Basking Ridge, NJ 07920 USA
https://www.TechnicsPub.com

Edited by Sadie Hoberman

Cover design by Lorena Molinari

First Printing 2021

Copyright © 2021 by Graham Witt

ISBN, print ed.	9781634629133
ISBN, Kindle ed.	9781634629140
ISBN, ePub ed.	9781634629157
ISBN, PDF ed.	9781634629164

Library of Congress Control Number: 2020952864

To Jessica, who left us too soon.

Acknowledgments

Sir Isaac Newton wrote in 1675: "If I have seen further, it is by standing on the shoulders of giants." I have many such giants to thank, in particular Chris Date, Harry Ellis, Michael Stonebraker, Bill Inmon, William Kent, and Terry Halpin.

I have also had the good fortune to have my imagination stimulated through collaboration and discussion with many in the international data modeling community, in particular Graeme Simsion, Geoff Bowles, Hu Schroor, John Giles, and Tim Woolford-Smith in Australia; David Hay, Fabian Pascal, and Dan Linstedt in the US; and Karen Lopez in Canada.

I must also thank those who both saw data modeling as important and trusted me to deliver quality to their clients. Graeme Simsion (again) not only invited me to join his consulting firm (Simsion Bowles & Associates), but trusted me to co-author the second and third editions of his seminal book *Data Modeling Essentials*. Geoff Howard (of AeM and later Ajilon) and David Hayward (of Ajilon) gave me opportunities to develop as a data modeler after my move to Sydney.

To be able to write this book I needed not only to practice my craft but explain it to others. Tony Shaw (of Dataversity), Jeremy Hall (of IRM UK), and Steve Hoberman (of Data Modeling Zone) each gave me many opportunities to do that at the conferences they organized in the US, the UK, and Germany.

To write a book as comprehensive as this was made a good deal easier with the support of family and friends – Isabel de Sousa, Brynnin Gilchrist, Gillian Essex and Mark Atkins – to all of whom I also owe thanks.

Finally a big thank you to Steve Hoberman (again) and Lorena Molinari at Technics Publications, who have been a pleasure to work with, both in making this book a reality and making the process as stress-free as possible.

.

Contents at a Glance

Contents

– Part 2: From requirements to an application fit for purpose –

Chapter 1.   Introduction

1.1   Objectives

This book is for all data modelers, data architects, and database designers—be they novices who want to learn what's involved in data modeling, or experienced modelers who want to brush up their skills. A novice will not only gain an overview of data modeling, they will also learn how to follow the data modeling process, including the activities required for each step. The experienced practitioner will discover (or rediscover) techniques to ensure that data models accurately reflect business requirements. In this book, all modelers will find:

- examples of real-world situations and the data structures that can be used to manage those situations

- appropriate and inappropriate models, the latter with reasons why

- multiple solutions to meet the same set of requirements, with the pros and cons of each solution

- a ready reference to dip into while modeling.

This book describes rigorous yet easily implemented approaches to:

- modeling of business information requirements for review by business stakeholders[1] before development of the logical data model

---

[1] These include potential users, their managers, and anyone else in the enterprise whose tasks will be supported by the proposed information resource.

- normalizing data, based on simple questions rather than the formal definitions which in my experience many modelers find intimidating

- naming and defining concepts and attributes

- modeling of time-variant data

- documenting business rules governing both the real world and data

- data modeling in an Agile project

- managing data model change in any type of project

- transforming a business information model to a logical data model against which developers can code

- implementing the logical data model in a traditional relational DBMS, an SQL:2003-compliant DBMS, an object-relational DBMS, or in XML.

This book also details several innovative data modeling approaches developed by the author and used successfully in complex projects. These include:

- attribute classes

- the use of a taxonomic glossary to support the naming of data model artifacts (entity classes, attributes, relationships)

- verbal description of a data model to communicate with business stakeholders ("the assertions technique")

- modeling XML data.

1.2   Topics

Part 1 describes **business information models** in-depth, including:

- the importance of modeling business information requirements before embarking on a **logical data model**

- **business concepts (entity classes)**

- **attributes** of business concepts

- **attribute classes** as an alternative to **DBMS data types**

- **relationships** between business concepts
- **time-variant** data
- **generalization** and **specialization** of business concepts
- **naming** and **defining** the components of the business information model
- **business rules** governing data, including a distinction between **real-world rules** and **data rules**.

Part 2 journeys from requirements to a working data resource, covering:

- sourcing data requirements
- developing the business information model
- communicating it to business stakeholders for review, both as diagrams and verbally
- managing data model change
- transforming the business information model into a **logical data model** of stored data for implementation in a **relational** or **object-relational** DBMS
- **attribute value representation** and **data constraints** (important but often overlooked)
- modeling **data vault**, **dimensional** and **XML** data.

1.3 Conventions

In this book:

- **bold sans serif** is used for the names of data model artifacts such as entity and object classes, attributes and attribute classes
- *italic sans serif* is used for relationship names
- normal sans serif on a grey background is used for data values, DBMS data types, and SQL operators and functions

- **bold serif** is used for each technical term relevant to data modeling (other than when mentioned in passing)[2]

- ***bold italic serif*** text is used for emphasis.

References to the real-world concepts being modeled (as distinct from the data model artifacts representing them) are in normal font but with initial capitals. For example:

- Order Item for the real-world concept

- **Order Item** for the entity class in the data model.

1.4   Abbreviations

The following abbreviations are used in this book:

- DBMS: Database Management System

- DDL: Data Definition Language

- ORM: Object-Role Modeling

- SQL: Structured Query Language

- UML: Unified Modeling Language

- XML: Extensible Markup Language.

---

[2] Unless its meaning is obvious from the context, each technical term is defined at a suitable point in the narrative. If necessary, other uses of technical terms are footnoted with a cross-reference to the section in which that term is defined.

1.5   What is a data model?

A data model is a description of a set of data to be used and/or maintained by an enterprise. That description inevitably involves words and is usually (but not necessarily) accompanied by one or more diagrams.

1.6   Why develop one?

Various authors have declared that data models are unnecessary. These include proponents of new technologies, such as XML and Big Data, as well as proponents of alternative approaches to system development, such as Agile.

The reality is, as my colleague Graeme Simsion stated in (Simsion & Witt, 2004), "No database was ever built without a model." He went on to say, "The choice is not whether or not to model, but (a) whether to do it formally, (b) whom to involve, and (c) how much effort to devote to producing a good design."

1.6.1   Use cases

Data models may be produced:

- as part of the design of a new application or data resource (e.g., data warehouse, XML message format)
- to document an undocumented existing application or data resource that is to be modified, to ensure that the modifications are appropriate and well-thought out
- to document an undocumented existing data resource that is to be the source of a data migration
- to provide a framework for system integration
- to provide an enterprise with a common understanding of its data.

1.6.2   Benefits

Producing a data model involves the expenditure of time and money but, if it is done properly, the benefits will outweigh the costs. The benefits of producing a quality data model vary according to purpose:

- If the model is being produced as part of the design of a new system or data resource, the principal benefit is that the system or resource will fulfill all business requirements in the most effective manner. Moreover, the time taken to develop the system or resource is likely to be reduced as rework resulting from misunderstandings is minimized.

- If the model is being produced to support modification of an undocumented system or data resource, the resulting modifications will meet requirements more effectively and take less time.

- If the model is being produced to support data migration from an undocumented data resource, development of the appropriate data migration logic will take less time.

- System integration is much easier to get right if the systems being integrated are documented by way of quality data models.

- A common understanding across an enterprise of the data that it uses is also much easier if a well-presented business-friendly data model has been produced.

Realization of these benefits depends on the quality of the model, the principal focus of this book.

1.6.3   Everyone's a data modeler

This statement is true only in the sense that everyone can sing. Even if someone can sing, that doesn't mean you would spend good money to hear them perform. I once started a conference presentation on data modeling by asking the delegates "who can play guitar?" The majority raised their hands, but when I then asked "who can play guitar really well?" only one hand stayed up (that of a semi-professional jazz guitarist).

It's much the same in the application development world. At the start of an assignment in which I was employed as Data Architect by the System Integrator, there was a planning meeting involving client representatives, the various software vendors, and the System Integrator team. The client's project manager asked, "who will be producing the data model?" The software vendors had previously agreed that, although they already had data models of their products, I would develop an integrated data model based on those models, in consultation with their people and appropriate client representatives, so they nodded when I identified myself. However, a number of client representatives then stated that they would also be producing data models. They eventually did so, but their models were of insufficient quality on which to base any serious design work.

1.7   Users

Business stakeholders use **business information models** (as described in Part 1 and defined in Chapter 9) to satisfy themselves that their data requirements have been understood. Developers use **logical data models** (as described in Chapter 11) as a source of object and attribute names, properties, and relationships to use in their code. Database administrators also use logical data models, as the basis of their work. Business information models can also be used by developers of **XML schemas** for communication protocols and industry data standards (as described in Chapter 12).

1.8   The importance of getting it right

Figure 1 depicts a novice modeler's attempt at a data model for a Student Administration system. Attributes marked in bold are **mandatory** (must be supplied for each Student). The markings at each end of the line between **Student** and **Class** indicate that a Student can only be assigned to one Class at a time whereas many Students can be assigned to the same Class.

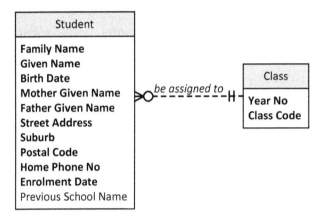

Figure 1: Student Administration data model (not recommended)

This model couldn't manage any of the following real-world scenarios:

- a Student's parent with a different family name from the Student (since there is only one **Family Name** attribute)

- a Student's parent residing at a different address from the Student (since there is only one set of address attributes: **Street Address**, **Suburb**, **Postal Code**)

- a Student's father being unknown or no longer involved in the Student's education (since **Father Given Name** is mandatory)

- a Student living with a two adults of the same gender, each having a parent/guardian role (since the only roles supported are Mother and Father)

- no home phone (since **Home Phone No** is mandatory).

I suspect this was because it was developed using a common but risky technique, that of *basing the model on only a small sample of real-world data.*

At the same time, it lacked support for what are nowadays considered to be essential requirements for a student administration system:

- emergency contact phone numbers, including the sequence in which to call those registered as emergency contacts for a Student (which may include people other than the Student's parents)

- if one of a Student's parents does not live with the Student, indications as to whether that parent

  o is wholly or partly liable for payment of school fees
  o receives academic reports
  o is invited to parent/teacher meetings
  o is allowed to pick the Student up from school

- the e-mail address of each parent/guardian, to support non-emergency contacts not delivered by mail.

This example illustrates two ways in which a model can be deficient:

- it lacks essential data (e.g., mobile phone numbers, e-mail addresses)

- it cannot manage the variety of scenarios that occur in real life.

We shall see later (in Section 6.7) a data model that manages all the listed scenarios and meets all the listed requirements.

1.9   Notation

There are three notation techniques in common use for diagramming data models:

- **Entity-Relationship Diagrams**[3], arguably the easiest notation to use and understand: there are many different styles, all of which use some form of box to represent each **entity class**[4] (often referred to simply as an **entity**) and a line to represent each **relationship**[5].

- **UML Class Diagrams**[6], which allow for some additional features, and which use a different nomenclature: **object class**[7] rather than entity class, and **association**[8] rather than relationship.

- **ORM Diagrams**[9], which provide many more features than either of the other two, at the cost of being less easily understood by those unfamiliar with the notation.

---

[3] An **Entity-Relationship Diagram** is a diagram of all or part of an **Entity-Relationship Model**, which uses **entity classes**, **attributes** and **relationships** to represent concepts of interest to an organization, their properties, and relationships.

[4] An **entity class** is an Entity-Relationship Model artifact that represents a class of people, places, things, or other concepts of interest to an enterprise.

[5] A **relationship** is a set of associations between instances of entity classes in an Entity-Relationship Model, e.g., '**Customer** *places* **Order**' is the set of instances of a Customer placing an Order.

[6] A **Class Diagram** is a diagram available in UML that describes a system's object classes, their attributes, and methods (operations) as well as associations between object classes.

[7] An **object class** is an artifact in a UML Class Diagram representing a class of people, places, things, or other concepts of interest to an enterprise.

[8] An **association** is the UML equivalent of a relationship in an Entity-Relationship Model.

[9] An **ORM Diagram** is the product of an Object-Role Modeling (ORM) exercise, depicting objects, the relationships between them, the roles that the objects play in those relationships, and constraints on objects and relationships.

Except where it is necessary to illustrate the options available in UML, the data model diagrams in this book are Entity-Relationship Diagrams using the same style as in Figure 1, in which:

- **mandatory attributes** are marked in bold, while **optional attributes**[10] are not

- markings on relationship lines have the meanings illustrated in Figure 2[11]

- a large circle is used to represent a set of **subtypes** and is linked to the boxes representing the subtypes and their **supertype** by plain lines with no marks, as also illustrated in Figure 2. This distinguishes them from lines representing relationships. Subtypes and supertypes are introduced and explained in Chapter 6.

---

[10] A **mandatory attribute** is one for which every instance of the entity class must have a value, whereas an **optional attribute** is one for which some instances of the entity class may not have a value.

[11] The meanings of relationship line markings are further detailed in Section 5.2.

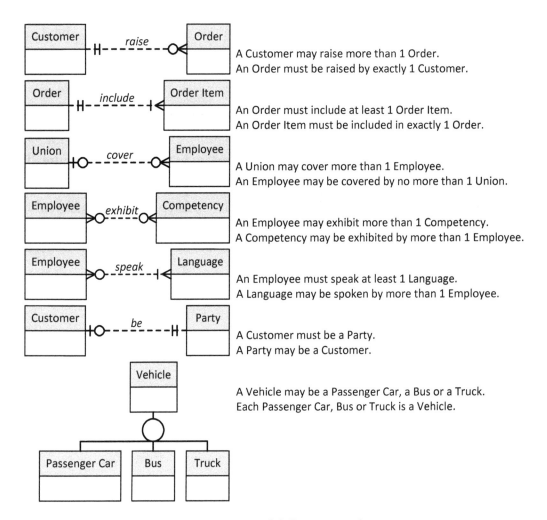

The figure contains the following relationship descriptions:

A Customer may raise more than 1 Order.
An Order must be raised by exactly 1 Customer.

An Order must include at least 1 Order Item.
An Order Item must be included in exactly 1 Order.

A Union may cover more than 1 Employee.
An Employee may be covered by no more than 1 Union.

An Employee may exhibit more than 1 Competency.
A Competency may be exhibited by more than 1 Employee.

An Employee must speak at least 1 Language.
A Language may be spoken by more than 1 Employee.

A Customer must be a Party.
A Party may be a Customer.

A Vehicle may be a Passenger Car, a Bus or a Truck.
Each Passenger Car, Bus or Truck is a Vehicle.

Figure 2: Data model diagram notation

Many data modeling tools support alternative styles of relationship marking. If the "crow's foot" style used in Figure 2 is available, I recommend you use it, as it is generally regarded as the most intuitive representation of "more than 1" or "at least 1". Do not be concerned if your data modeling tool uses a different style for entity class boxes.

— Part 1 —

Business information models

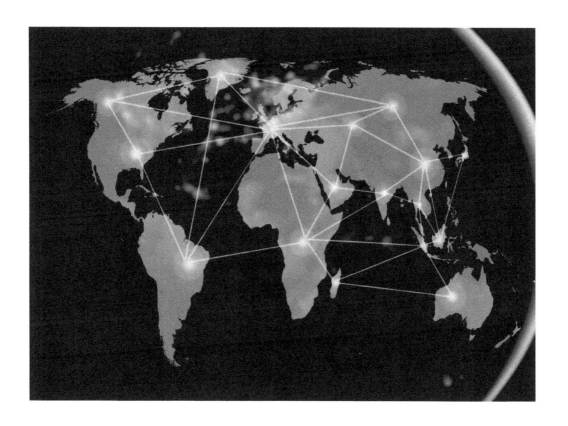

Chapter 2.   Modeling business information requirements

I am occasionally asked why this step is necessary—the implication being that all that is required are logical and physical data models, and possibly a high-level model conveying relatively little information.

2.1   Why not develop the logical data model immediately?

Many developers prefer to get started on a logical data model so they can start coding. However, a suitable logical data model can't be developed until the business information requirements are understood and documented in a manner that business stakeholders can understand.

The resulting model is a **business information model**[12], consisting of:

- **business concepts**[13] (**concepts** for short), each with **attributes**[14], each attribute belonging to an **attribute class**[15]

- **relationships**[16] between **concepts**.

---

[12] Business information models are defined in Chapter 9.

[13] Business concepts are described in Chapter 3.

[14] Attributes are described in Chapter 4.

[15] Attribute classes are described in Section 4.7.

[16] Relationships are described in Chapter 5.

I prefer this term to **conceptual data model**, which has so many different definitions that it has become useless for any meaningful discourse.

2.2   Why not document requirements using a logical data model?

If a system is to support an enterprise's business information requirements, a necessary step in its design is an effective review of that design by appropriate business stakeholders. For such a review to be effective, the design documentation provided to those stakeholders must:

- be understandable

- be complete (include *all* information in which business stakeholders are interested)

- *not* include any information in which business stakeholders have no interest (such information acts as "noise", with potential to distract or confuse reviewers, thus reducing review effectiveness).

A logical data model is not suitable as a business information model, since it describes the precise structure of a database and the meaning of its components to three audiences:

- *database developer*(s), so that the database is built as required

- *application developers*, so that code accurately populates and updates the database

- *report developers*, so that reports accurately interpret database content.

Thus a logical data model is likely to fail both the understandability criterion and the "no noise" criterion.

Figure 3 illustrates an effective data modeling process designed to ensure that the resulting database design supports business requirements.

This process works well even for an **Agile** project, but with multiple short iterations, as discussed in Section 10.4.1.

One key to the success of this process is the ease with which a business information model can be transformed into a logical data model, as discussed in Chapter 11.

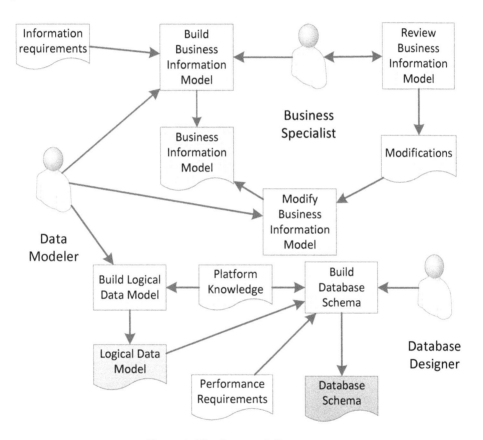

Figure 3: The data modeling process

2.3   Summary

If a system is to support an enterprise's business information requirements, those requirements need to be documented for review by business stakeholders. This is best achieved by a model that:

- is understandable
- includes all information in which business stakeholders are interested
- does not include any information in which business stakeholders have no interest.

A logical data model is not suitable as a business information model, since it describes the precise structure of a database to developers.

Chapter 3.   Business concepts

Broadly speaking, a **business concept** (or **concept**) is any class of things about which the enterprise sees value in storing and retrieving information. Each concept represents a set of similar real-world instances of people (or other animals) or concrete or abstract things.

Each participant in discussion of a concept will have a mental picture of that concept, which may focus on either a representative individual instance or the common features of instances of that concept. For example, if the concept being discussed is **Vehicle**, the business stakeholders may each be thinking of their own car, whereas the data modeler may be thinking about what makes something a vehicle rather than something else, like a boat. That isn't a problem, but to make life easier down the track, we will follow accepted convention and refer to each concept with a singular name (**Vehicle** instead of **Vehicles**), even though that name is understood to represent *all* vehicles.

A business concept may represent any of the following:

- **Parties** playing some role with respect to the enterprise:
    - persons, e.g., **Employee**, **Salesperson**
    - formal or informal organizations, e.g., **Regulator**, **Organization Unit**, **Project Team**
    - informal groups of persons or organizations, e.g., **Household**
    - roles played by persons or organizations, e.g., **Customer**, **Supplier**

- **Products** or **Services** that the enterprise supplies, e.g., **Product**, **Warranty**, **Service**

- **Agreements** between the enterprise and some other party, e.g., **Employment Contract**, **Maintenance Contract**, **Customer Account**

- **Events** involving the enterprise, e.g., **Order**, **Delivery**, **Service Call**, **Customer Communication**

- **Locations** in which the enterprise, its customers, or its suppliers operate or reside, e.g., **Country**, **City**, **Address**, **Building**, **Office**, **Meeting Room**

- **Physical Resources** used by the enterprise, its customers, or its suppliers, e.g., **Equipment Item**, **Vehicle**

- **Financial Arrangements** used by the enterprise, its customers, or its suppliers, e.g., **Bank Account**, **General Ledger Account**.

Most enterprises will find that these seven top-level concepts—and the more specific concepts they embrace—cover their business information requirements, but others can be added as required. For example, many enterprises find **Organizational Concept** useful, as it can include such things as ways of dividing up the enterprise's operations for organizational or reporting purposes (e.g., **Region**, **Market Segment**).

A variation on this list of top-level concepts appears in Section 7.4.2.

Note that we only need to consider those concepts that the enterprise is sufficiently interested to invest in storing and retrieving data about.

3.1   Role concepts

Some concepts reflect roles played by persons or organizations (or, occasionally, other concepts). For example, **Customer** and **Supplier** are two roles of interest to most enterprises. While some persons or organizations may be only **Customers** and others may be only **Suppliers**, some may be both. Similarly some persons may be only **Customers**, and some may be only **Employees**, but others may be both.

It is acceptable in a business information model to just create a concept for each role of interest, but this involves creating a largely similar set of **attributes**[17] for each concept. The resulting duplication (illustrated in Figure 4) increases effort and the likelihood of inconsistency. A better alternative is to add a **Party** concept to represent the Persons and Organizations themselves and a relationship between **Party** and each role concept (as illustrated in Figure 5). We now only have 13 attributes to deal with rather than 21.

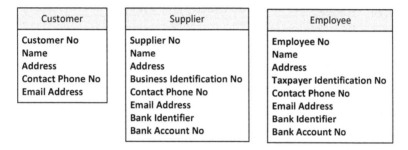

Figure 4: Role concepts

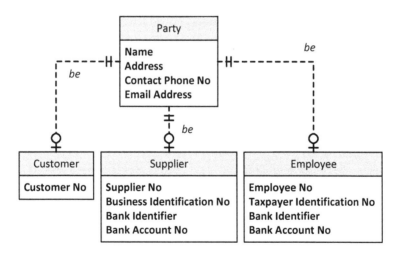

Figure 5: Roles played by Parties

---

[17] **Attributes** are properties of concepts, and are discussed in detail in Chapter 4.

Note the relationship markings at each end, which communicate:

- Any given **Party** may *be* exactly one **Customer** (but may not be).
- Any given **Party** may *be* exactly one **Supplier** (but may not be).
- Any given **Party** may *be* exactly one **Employee** (but may not be).
- Any given **Customer** must *be* exactly one **Party**.
- Any given **Supplier** must *be* exactly one **Party**.
- Any given **Employee** must *be* exactly one **Party**.

Note that this set of relationships doesn't prevent a Party from playing more than one role, e.g., being a Customer as well as a Supplier, which is what we want. However, it also doesn't prevent a Party from playing none of these roles. It is up to the business to decide whether that is a permissible state of affairs. If it isn't, we will have to document the requirement that each Party must play at least one role (as discussed in Section 8.4.3).

Some things about these models may need some further consideration:

- The **Name** attribute has a different form for persons and organizations, and may require more than just a single attribute.
- **Address** may also require more than just a single attribute.
- Only **Persons** can play the **Employee** role, whereas both **Persons** and **Organizations** can play the **Customer** and **Supplier** roles.

We shall deal with these considerations in due course[18].

---

[18] **Composite attributes** such **Person Name** and **Address** are discussed in Section 4.4. Modeling the types of party that can play each role is discussed in Section 6.4.

3.2   Persistent roles and event roles

The **Customer**, **Supplier**, and **Employee** roles are **persistent roles**, in that most Parties play those roles for multiple transactions over time.

By contrast, **event roles** are those that a Party plays for a specific event, such as the various roles played in a lawsuit (**Plaintiff**, **Defendant**, **Witness**, **Prosecuting Attorney**, **Defending Attorney**, **Judge**, **Jury Member**, etc.).

3.3   Documenting concepts

If you are using an Entity-Relationship modeling tool, each concept should be documented as an **entity class** (**entity** for short).

If you are using a UML tool, each concept should be documented as an **object class**.

3.4   Summary

A **business concept** is any class of similar real-world instances of people or concrete or abstract things about which the enterprise sees value in storing and retrieving information.

Each concept is given a singular rather than plural name.

A concept may represent a set of parties (persons or organizations), products, services, agreements, events, locations, physical resources, financial arrangements, or other organizational concepts used by the enterprise, its customers, or its suppliers.

Some concepts reflect roles played by persons or organizations. Distinguishing Parties from the Roles they play enables us to model Parties who play more than one Role.

Persistent roles are those (such as Customer, Supplier and Employee), which a Party may play on an ongoing basis, whereas **event roles** are those that a Party plays for a specific event.

Chapter 4.   Attributes of concepts

Each instance of a concept of interest to the enterprise (e.g., each **Customer**, each **Product**, or each **Order**) has various attributes that:

- identify it (e.g., **Customer Name**, **Product Code**, **Order Number**), or

- describe it (e.g., the **Gender** or **Birth Date** of a **Customer**; the **Description**, **Weight**, or **Unit Price** of a **Product**; the **Delivery Date** of an **Order**).

Note that the modeler only needs to itemize those attributes of sufficient interest to the enterprise to be worth the investment in storing and retrieving information about them. In deciding whether to include an attribute, the question to ask is, "would we expect to see this attribute represented in a user interface or web page?" Thus the **Hair Color** of a Customer would not be included (unless the enterprise is a hair salon or supplier of hair products, or a law enforcement agency—which might wish to record the hair color of each Person of Interest).

The modeler should avoid making assumptions about what the enterprise is interested in. When I started data modeling, it was common for personnel systems (as Human Resources systems were called then) to record the birth date of each employee, but that is generally no longer the case (at least in Australia). It is still common for such systems to record the home address of each employee. However—to my surprise—the first personnel system I built did not require home addresses. This was because no mail was ever sent to an employee's home address, and many of the home addresses that had been recorded on cards were out of date as there was no incentive for either the enterprise or the employees to keep them up to date.

4.1   Does a business information model need attributes?

There is a school of thought which sees attributes as being unnecessary in a data model presented to business stakeholders. However, before we can confidently proceed to develop a logical data model, we need agreement on what attributes are required.

If the stakeholders have an appetite for multiple review cycles, it's fine to *start* with an attribute-free model and present that to stakeholders before adding attributes. In that case, the final model to be reviewed must include *all* attributes that will be visible to users of the delivered application.

Of course, if the model is merely to provide a common enterprise-wide understanding of the data that it uses (and not for any of the other purposes listed in Section 1.6.1), it *may* have some value without attributes.

If you are using an Entity-Relationship modeling tool, each attribute should be documented as an **attribute** of the **entity class** representing the relevant concept. If you are using a UML tool, each attribute should be documented as an **attribute** of the **object class** representing the relevant concept.

4.2   Normalization

A data modeling project inevitably has to deal with **normalization**, by which attributes are assigned to the right entity classes. Much of the advice available on this topic, online and in books, is rather complicated and intimidating. Assigning an attribute to the appropriate concept can be confidently done in a relatively intuitive manner, which I shall illustrate by example.

Consider the data required to capture details of Orders by Customers for Products sold by the enterprise. Figure 6 depicts a **flat file**[19] of Order data.

Order Item
Order No
Order Date
Customer No
Customer Name
Delivery Address
Delivery Date
Product Code
Product Description
Unit Price
Order Quantity

Figure 6: Order data as a flat file

If this were implemented as such in a relational database, it could look something like Figure 7.

Order No	Order Date	Customer No	Customer Name	Delivery Address	Delivery Date	Product Code	Product Description	Unit Price	Order Quantity
5678	1/10/20	123	Alf Price	7 New St, Newtown 2345	16/10/20	BAA6	AA Battery 6 Pack	$5	100
5678	1/10/20	123	Alf Price	7 New St, Newtown 2345	16/10/20	BAAA6	AAA Battery 6 Pack	$4.50	100
5678	1/10/20	123	Alf Price	7 New St, Newtown 2345	16/10/20	LB182	18W Lightbulb 2 Pack	$15.30	50
5679	1/10/20	456	Fred Bare	9 Old St, Oldham 2678	23/10/20	LB182	18W Lightbulb 2 Pack	$15.30	50
5680	2/10/20	123	Alf Price	7 New St, Newtown 2345	17/10/20	LB232	23W Lightbulb 2 Pack	$19.90	20

Figure 7: Order data in a relational database

Note that there is some repetition of data:

- Each row for **Order No** 5678 has the same **Order Date**, **Customer No**, **Customer Name**, **Delivery Address**, and **Delivery Date**.

- Each row for **Product Code** LB182 has the same **Product Description**, **Unit Price**, and **Order Quantity**.

- Each row for **Customer No** 123 has the same **Customer Name** and **Delivery Address**.

---

[19] A **flat file** is a single file or table used to hold information which might alternatively be held in a more complex structure.

Is this repetition simply coincidence or is it inevitable? Although you would expect the Product Description to be the same for each instance of a particular Product Code, there is no reason why every order for a particular product should be for the same Quantity. We can therefore write the repetition of **Order Quantity** down to coincidence.

What about **Delivery Address** and **Delivery Date**? Let's assume for the moment that if a customer wants products delivered to different addresses or on different dates, they have to raise separate Orders. If this is the case, all other repetitions are inevitable.

Moreover, these repetitions create the risk of **update anomalies**, which can arise whenever an attribute appears in multiple rows of a database table but should have the same value in each row. If one or more instances of that attribute are updated but not others, the database is no longer consistent.

For example, **Order Date** could be updated in some rows in which **Order No** is 5678 but not other rows with the same Order No. If we now query the database to find out when Order 5678 was raised, multiple dates will be returned.

Similarly, **Product Description** could be updated in some rows in which **Product Code** is LB182 but not other rows with the same **Product Code**. If we now query the database for the description of Product LB182, multiple descriptions will be returned.

We need to avoid that risk, so we need to **normalize** the data model. How can we do that?

4.2.1   Functional dependency

Let's revisit the repetition of data that we observed in Figure 7:

- More than one row can have the same **Order No** (e.g., 5678). This is appropriate, as we want Customers to be able to order more than one Product in the same Order.

- Each row with the same **Order No** should have:

    ○ the same **Order Date**, as there is only one date on which a particular Order is raised

    ○ the same **Customer No** and **Customer Name**, as only one Customer can raise an Order

    ○ the same **Delivery Address** and **Delivery Date**, as Products delivered to different Addresses or on different Dates should be on separate Orders.

- More than one row can have the same **Product Code** (e.g., LB182). This is appropriate as we want our Products to be ordered more than once.

- Each row with the same **Product Code** should have the same **Product Description** and **Unit Price** but not necessarily the same **Order Quantity**.

- More than one row can have the same **Customer No** (e.g., 123). This is appropriate as we want our Customers to be able to raise multiple Orders.

- Each row with the same **Customer No** should have the same **Customer Name** but not necessarily the same **Delivery Address**.

These are examples of **functional dependencies**:

- **Order Date, Customer No, Customer Name, Delivery Address**, and **Delivery Date** are each **functionally dependent** on **Order No**

- **Product Description** and **Unit Price** are each functionally dependent on **Product Code**

- **Customer Name** is functionally dependent on **Customer No.**

Moreover, **Order No**, **Product Code**, and **Customer No** are each **non-unique** in this table, meaning that more than one row of this table can have the same value of any of these attributes.

If an entity class has any attributes that are *functionally dependent on a non-unique attribute*, it is not in **3rd Normal Form**[20].

Thus there are two questions we should ask about each attribute of an entity class:

1. Is this attribute functionally dependent on some other attribute, i.e., is it necessarily the same in each row in which the other attribute has a particular value?

2. Can that other attribute have the same value in multiple instances of this entity class?

The answer to both these questions is "Yes" for:

- **Order Date**, **Customer No**, **Customer Name**, **Delivery Address**, and **Delivery Date**, which are functionally dependent on the non-unique **Order No**

- **Product Description** and **Unit Price**, which are functionally dependent on the non-unique **Product Code**

- **Customer Name**, which is functionally dependent on the non-unique **Customer No**.

Note that **Customer Name** appears to be dependent on both **Order No** and **Customer No**. Whenever an attribute appears to be dependent on more than one other attribute, it may simply be dependent on one attribute which is in turn dependent on another. In this case, **Customer Name** is dependent on **Customer**

---

[20] It is not in **Boyce-Codd Normal Form** either, but **3rd Normal Form** is the more commonly-known property. An entity class is in 3rd Normal Form if every attribute is functionally dependent on only a unique attribute.

No, which is in turn dependent on **Order No**. In this situation we ignore the indirect dependency (in this case that of **Customer Name** on **Order No**).

Since **Order No** appears to identify Orders, **Customer Name** appears to identify Customers, and **Product Code** appears to identify Products, we should add **Order**, **Customer**, and **Product** entity classes, and move each set of dependent attributes and the attribute on which that set depends to the appropriate new entity class, as illustrated in Figure 8.

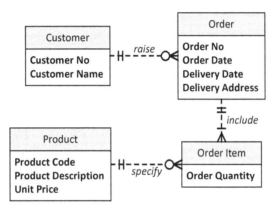

Figure 8: Order, Customer, and Product attributes moved to separate entity classes

However, there is a serious problem with this model: the unit price of a Product may change after an Order is raised, but the price charged for that Product in that Order should remain the same as when the Order was raised. To achieve this, we need to record the Unit Price at the time the Order was raised, as well as the current Unit Price, so we need to add a **Unit Price** attribute to the **Order Item** entity class, as in Figure 9.

Where are we now? The model is in **3rd Normal Form**, and we have catered for price changes after Orders are raised. Before we consider the job done, we should ask whether this model supports a flexible way of doing business. What if some Customers would like to request that some Items within the one Order be delivered on different dates and/or to different delivery addresses (rather than having to raise multiple Orders)?

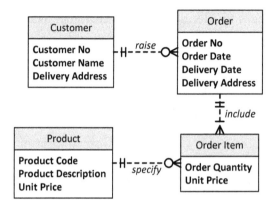

Figure 9: Corrected model, with Price at the time the Order was raised

If the enterprise has an appetite for providing Customers with this flexibility, the simplest approach is to move **Delivery Date** from **Order** to **Order Item** and **Delivery Address** from **Customer** to **Order Item**. However, many Customers want most Items delivered to the same address, so we should leave a **Delivery Address** attribute (renamed **Normal Delivery Address**) in **Customer**, as in Figure 10.

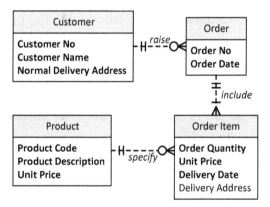

Figure 10: Flexible delivery

Note that **Delivery Address** in **Order Item** is optional, since it only needs to be specified for Items to be delivered to other than the **Normal Delivery Address**.

The model in Figure 10 is actually in **Boyce-Codd Normal Form**[21]. This particular model cannot be further normalized. However, there is another normal form which *may* be appropriate for models in which there is a requirement to record history. This is discussed in Section 11.12.5.

4.2.2   Why are there no foreign keys?

If you're already familiar with data models, you may well wonder why there are no foreign keys in any of the data models in Section 4.2.1. This is deliberate:

- While foreign keys are the only way to implement a relationship in a traditional **relational DBMS**[22], there are other ways to do so in an **SQL:2003**[23] DBMS, an **object-relational DBMS**[24], and **XML**[25].

- These are *business information models*: business stakeholders generally aren't interested in implementation alternatives.

- If the business information model is to be effectively reviewed, it should contain no extraneous information. Representing each relationship by both a line and an attribute marked as a foreign key is redundant and clutters up the diagram.

---

[21] An entity class is in **Boyce-Codd Normal Form** if all redundancy based on functional dependency has been removed. This and most other normal forms are discussed in depth in (Simsion & Witt, 2004).

[22] A **relational DBMS** is one that organizes data in accordance with the **relational model**, in tables consisting of columns and rows, each table having a unique key by which rows are identified, and with rows being associated with each other by way of references to another row's key.

[23] **SQL:2003** is the 2003 update of the 1999 **SQL:99** standard (now deprecated), which added a number of features not present in the original 1986 standard. Although later versions of the SQL standard have been published in 2006, 2008, 2011, and 2016, the 2003 version is the earliest extant version to support all the features used in this book. Different vendors support different subsets of the 2003 and later standards.

[24] An **object-relational DBMS** supports both object-oriented and relational features.

[25] **XML** is described in Chapter 12.

- Some data modeling tools automatically create a foreign key column when a relationship line is drawn but give you the option of hiding it.

4.2.3   Functional dependency on more than one attribute

Consider Figure 11, in which **Make**, **Model**, **Number Of Seats**, **Number Of Doors**, and **Transmission** are functionally dependent on the combination of **State Code** and **Registration No**, which can have the same values in multiple instances (the same Vehicle can be rented multiple times).

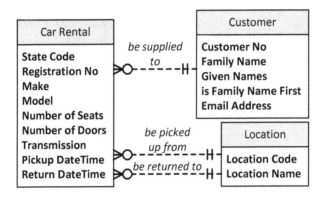

Figure 11: Car rental

This model should be normalized in a similar way to that described in Section 4.2.1, by:

- adding a new entity class (**Vehicle**)

- moving **State Code**, **Registration No**, **Make**, **Model**, **Number Of Seats**, **Number Of Doors**, and **Transmission** to the new entity class

- drawing a relationship from **Vehicle** to **Car Rental**.

4.2.4   Functional dependency on a relationship

Consider Figure 12, which could have resulted from the transformation of the model in Figure 6 (instead of Figure 10). However, this has two attributes that are functionally dependent on relationships:

1. **Customer No** in **Order** should always have the same value as **Customer No** in the related **Customer**. If it doesn't, we have inconsistent data (unless the business model is that Customers can raise Orders for each other).

2. **Product Code** in **Order Item** should always have the same value as **Product Code** in the related **Product**. Again, if it doesn't, we have inconsistent data.

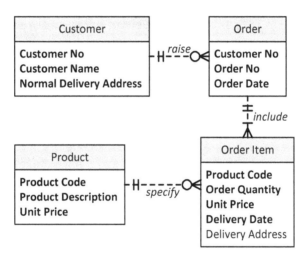

Figure 12: Functional dependencies on relationships

What we have here in each case is a *functional dependency on a relationship*, which in a business information model means the model is not yet in 3rd Normal Form. In fact, **Customer No** in **Order** and **Product Code** in **Order Item** are **redundant**, and should be removed, to produce the model in Figure 10.

Note that *in a logical data model*, the appearance of **Product Code** in both **Product** and **Order Item** would not indicate a non-3rd Normal Form model *if* **Product Code** were the **primary key** of **Product** and a **foreign key** in **Order Item**.

However, business information models do *not* include primary and foreign keys, which are a relationship implementation technique of no interest to business stakeholders.

My aside (that Customers can raise Orders for each other) raises the question, "can Customers raise Orders for recipients other than themselves?" While the earliest ordering systems did not support this, it is now a common facility in mail order systems, which provide an easy means of sending gifts to friends and relatives. The Recipient should not have to be a Customer, so, by adding **Recipient Name** and **Recipient Address** to Order, we now have a model for mail order (Figure 13). **Recipient Name** and **Recipient Address** are both optional since, if a Customer is ordering for themself, **Recipient Name** and **Recipient Address** are left blank, and the **Customer Name** and **Normal Delivery Address** are used.

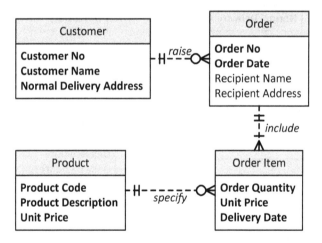

Figure 13: Mail order

One final note before we move on from this model. You may have noticed that the relationships between **Customer** and **Order**, and between **Product** and **Order Item**, are optional at the n end, whereas the relationship between **Order** and **Order Item** is mandatory at the n end. This is because Customers are retained in the database even though they may have no current Orders, and Products may exist for which there are no current Orders. However, an Order must include at least one Order Item.

4.3   Derived attributes

All attributes that the business stakeholders expect to see in a user interface or web page should be included even if they can be derived from other attributes. For example, the Total Value of an Order and the Extension for each Order Item (the Quantity multiplied by the Unit Price) are usually displayed to the customer and to sales staff.

When including derived attributes, you should indicate in some way that each of them is derived from other attributes, and document the derivation formula. In this case, the formulae are:

- **Extension = Order Quantity × Unit Price**
- **Total Order Value** = sum(**Extension**).

Your data modeling tool may provide an option for marking attributes as derived and documenting the derivation formulae. Make sure that there is some indication on the data model diagram that particular attributes are derived.

If the tool does not provide such an option, then:

1. Check whether the tool allows non-alphabetic characters in attribute names. If it does,
   - agree with the business stakeholders what character to use as a prefix or suffix in the name of each derived attribute, such as the oblique ('/'), used in UML class models to mark derived attributes
   - include the agreed character in the attribute name
2. Include the derivation formula for each derived attribute in the definition of the attribute (see Section 7.5.2).

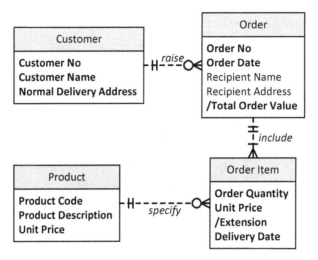

Figure 14: Derived attributes

4.4   Composite attributes

4.4.1   Addresses

I was once in charge of a data modeling exercise for a client, leading a team of competent modelers. On my first day on the project I had to undertake various administrative tasks, so I got the team to spend the morning reading the business requirements specification and the afternoon modeling a requirement that would be relatively easy to model. During the afternoon, I dropped by to see how they were doing, and found that they had decided to model street addresses.

This was understandable since they all knew what a street address looked like, but they had become bogged down in arguments such as:

- Should each street address consist of

  - ○ separate attributes for **Unit No**, **Street No**, **Street Name**, **Street Type**, **Street Suffix** (e.g., 'East', 'West'), **Locality Name**, **State/Province/County Name**, **Postal Code**[26], **Country Name**?
  - ○ separate **Address Line 1**, **Address Line 2**, …, **Address Line** *n* attributes?
  - ○ some combination of the above, such as **Address Line 1**, **Address Line 2**, **Locality Name**, **State/Province/County Name**, **Postal Code**, **Country Name**?

- What about Post Office Box addresses?

To make matters worse, addresses were to be found in multiple existing systems with varying formats and, although Australia Post (the Australian postal service) had published a standard for address data, the business didn't seem keen to use that standard rather than one of their existing formats. My advice was to defer these considerations until we could consult with business stakeholders, and meanwhile model each address as a simple **Address** attribute, this being a business information model.

This gave us some flexibility. If the business stakeholders agreed on a particular address format before the conclusion of business information model development, we could document that in the business information model, as described below. If, on the other hand, they had not yet agreed on an address format by then, the breakdown of addresses into separate attributes could be deferred to the logical data model.

----

[26] e.g., **Zip Code** in the US, **Postcode** in Australia.

Another advantage of this approach was that it avoided the situation I had encountered in another project, in which addresses were scattered throughout the model. A decision was then made to change address formats, and all but one occurrence of the addresses in the model were changed.

By contrast, in this project, we had a single place in the model in which address formats were defined.

4.4.2   Documenting composite attributes

So how do we document address formats?

UML tools support **user-defined data types**, both simple and composite, so, if you are using a UML tool, you can create an **Address** data type, as illustrated in Figure 15.

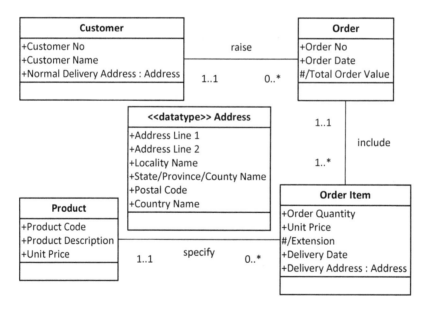

Figure 15: Address data type in UML

Ignore the '+' and '#' symbols next to attribute names. This is implementation information which is irrelevant in a business information model, but few if any

UML tools provide a means to hide these symbols. Also, ignore for the moment the '1..1', '0..*' and '1..*' annotations: these are discussed in Section 5.2.

Although most (if not all) Entity-Relationship modeling tools support user-defined data types (as **domains**[27]), I'm not aware of any that support composite data types. There are two options for documenting a composite attribute in an Entity-Relationship Model[28], neither of them ideal:

1. Create an **Address** domain and list its components (**Unit Number**, **Street Number**, etc.) in whatever free text **metadata**[29] field is provided by the tool to describe a domain. Associate each **Address** attribute with that domain using its **attribute class** (see Section 4.7). This adds to the conversion work when creating the logical data model from the business information model but has the advantage that the business information model remains relatively simple (see Figure 16).

2. Create an **Address** entity class in the business information model to represent all addresses and add a relationship between the **Address** entity class and each entity class that has an address (see Figure 17). This makes the business information model rather more complex, but has the following advantages:

   o It simplifies creation of the logical data model from the business information model but *only* if we decide at that stage to hold addresses in a separate table.

---

[27] The term **domain** is one of the most over-used terms in the IT field. In addition to its meanings in various fields of mathematics, it is variously used to refer to a) the set of values of an attribute, b) a subject area, and c) part of a website address.

[28] Note the distinction between **Entity-Relationship Diagram** and **Entity-Relationship Model**: only some aspects of an Entity-Relationship Model are shown in a corresponding Entity-Relationship Diagram.

[29] **Metadata** is data about data.

- o It exposes the chosen address structure to business stakeholders, and is therefore more likely to prompt feedback if we've chosen an inappropriate structure.

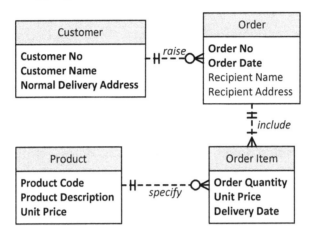

Figure 16: Addresses as attributes

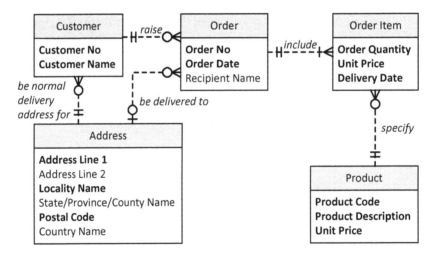

Figure 17: Addresses as an entity class

Note that holding addresses as a separate table (as is implied in Figure 17) requires careful handling of changes of address. This is because the implied structure allows multiple parties to have the same address. This can be useful in a school administration system, for example, as the cost of postage can be saved where a student and their parents live at the same address. However, if any family member notifies a change of address, the address record itself must not be updated unless *all* family members in the system are moving to the new address. Address updating should proceed as follows:

1. establish which people currently at the old address are moving to the new address

2. create a new address row and link each person identified in step 1 to that new row

3. delete the old address row if and only if all people currently at the old address are moving to the new address.

4.4.3   Other composite attributes

There are many other composite attributes, including:

- **Person Names**, which consist of a **Title** (Mr, Ms, Dr, Prof, etc.), one or more **Given Names**, a **Family Name**, optional **Post-Nominal** (e.g., PhD), and ideally an attribute indicating whether the family name appears first or last[30]

- **Phone Numbers**, which consist of a **Country Code**, **Area Code**, and **Local Number**

- **Date Ranges**, which consist of a **Start Date** and **End Date**

- **Balances** in multi-currency accounts, which consist of a **Currency** and a **Monetary Amount**.

Note that it would not make sense to model any of these as separate entity classes, the only possible exception being date ranges, and then only if the only

---

[30] See Section 6.6.2 for my reasoning behind the inclusion of this attribute.

date ranges that occurred were pre-defined ranges such as Accounting Periods, Calendar Months, Financial Years, or Financial Quarters.

4.5   Multi-valued attributes

An attribute may hold multiple values of the same type for any given instance of a concept. For example, a **Scheduled Flight** in an airline timetable has two such attributes:

- **Days of Operation** (the set of days of the week on which that Flight operates)
- **Meals** (the set of meals served during that Flight).

This is illustrated in Figure 18, in which the only indication that **Days of Operation** and **Meals** are multi-valued is that they are plural noun phrases rather than the singular noun phrases normally employed for attribute names. By contrast, UML allows the **multiplicity**[31] of an attribute to be displayed in a class diagram (see **Balance** in **Account** in Figure 22 in Section 4.6).

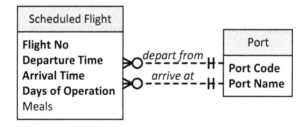

Figure 18: Flight Schedule with multi-valued attributes

---

[31] The **multiplicity** of an attribute is equivalent to the cardinality of a relationship, i.e., how many instances of the attribute may occur in one instance of the object class.

If you are familiar with normalization, you may wonder why I allow these attributes. Firstly, multi-valued attributes are ubiquitous in application system design:

- they were introduced in the **SQL:99** standard in 1999 and retained in the **SQL:2003** standard[32]

- they are supported in many modern **relational** and **object-relational** DBMSs[33] as well as **XML**[34]

- they are supported in **UML**[35] and **object-oriented programming**[36].

Secondly, a data model can be in **3rd Normal Form**[37] (or even a higher normal form) without being in **1st Normal Form**[38]. In fact, 1st Normal Form is only required in a physical data model where either:

- the target platform does not support multi-valued attributes, or

- it does but the database designer chooses not to exploit that capability, e.g., for performance reasons.

---

[32] **SQL:99** and **SQL:2003** are discussed in Section 4.2.2.

[33] **Relational** and **object-relational** DBMSs are defined in Section 4.2.2.

[34] **XML** is described in Chapter 12.

[35] **UML** is an object-oriented modeling approach supporting a variety of model types, including **object class models** (used in many enterprises as an alternative to **Entity-Relationship Models**), represented as **class diagrams** (defined in Section 1.9).

[36] **Object-oriented programming** is a programming paradigm based on the concept of objects, which can contain not only data but procedure code ("methods"), and which exhibit awareness of themselves and other objects.

[37] A table is in **3rd Normal Form** if every column is functionally dependent on only a unique identifier.

[38] A table is in **1st Normal Form** if it contains no "repeating groups" (columns which have sets of values rather than single values). This definition (by Edgar Codd) is generally extended by practitioners to include also **non-atomic values** (such as multiple telephone numbers separated by spaces or commas in a single column) and multiple columns each containing values of the same type (e.g., **Telephone Number 1**, **Telephone Number 2**, and so on).

The 1st Normal Form model of the same data is illustrated in Figure 19. It uses more graphic artifacts to depict the same information as Figure 18, so is less suitable for review by business stakeholders.

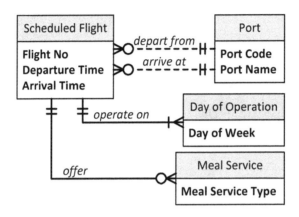

Figure 19: Flight Schedule with separate dependent entity classes

Note that the relationship lines between **Scheduled Flight** and the dependent entity classes are solid rather than dashed. This is to indicate that these three entity classes between them represent a single concept (the dependent entity classes representing multi-valued attributes of **Scheduled Flight**) rather than related concepts like **Port** and **Scheduled Flight**. Do not be concerned if your data modeling tool does not allow this distinction (which is useful but not essential).

4.5.1   Independent and coupled multi-valued attributes

The attributes **Days of Operation** and **Meals** in Figure 18 are independent, in that there is no association between Days of Operation and Meals: different Meals may be served on different Flights with the same Days of Operation, and different Flights on which the same Meals are served may have different Days of Operation.

By contrast, Figure 20 depicts a model of an entire Order as a single entity class with four multi-valued attributes: **Product Codes**, **Product Descriptions**, **Unit Prices**, and **Order Quantities**. These four attributes are **coupled**: each Product Description, Unit Price, and Order Quantity is associated with a single Product Code. However, there is no way to establish which Product Code a Product Description, Unit Price, or Order Quantity is associated with.

Order
Order No
Order Date
Customer Name
Delivery Address
Delivery Date
Product Codes
Product Descriptions
Unit Prices
Order Quantities

Figure 20: Order data with multi-valued attributes (not recommended)

The only way to maintain the association between these attributes would be to create a single multi-valued composite attribute Order Items, each value of which would consist of a Product Code, Product Description, Unit Price, and Order Quantity. Multi-valued composite attributes (and how to model them) are discussed in Section 4.6.

4.5.2   Sequence in a multi-valued attribute

The values of a multi-valued attribute of a given entity instance should be displayed in any user interface (or report) in a consistent logical sequence.

For some multi-valued attributes (like **Days of Operation**), the required sequence is fixed. However, it is still necessary to establish whether Sunday should be displayed at the start or end—for instance, should it be Sunday, Wednesday, Friday or Wednesday, Friday, Sunday? Once that requirement is understood, the sequence can be considered as an intrinsic property of the days of the week, which can be ensured by way of a suitable internal representation (see Section

11.7.1.5). That representation will be documented in the logical data model. However, since the preferred sequence should be identified during the business information model development, it should be documented in the appropriate attribute definition (see Section 7.5.2) in the business information model.

For other multi-valued attributes (like **Meals**), the sequence should be the sequence in which meals are served. However, this will vary from Flight to Flight: on some long-haul overnight flights leaving before midday, lunch, dinner, and breakfast are served in that sequence, whereas on some early morning flights, breakfast is served before lunch. Again, the requirement for a time-based sequence should be documented in the attribute definition. The addition of a sequence number in the logical data model is discussed in Section 11.10.2.

4.5.3   Functional dependency and multi-valued attributes

In Section 4.2.1, I introduced the topic of functional dependency, and stated that a model is not in 3rd Normal Form if:

1. an entity class has an attribute that always has the same value when some other attribute has the same value, and

2. that other attribute can have the same value in multiple instances of the entity class.

In Section 4.2.4, I stated that a model is not in 3rd Normal Form if an entity class has an attribute that always has the same value as an attribute in a related entity class (one that is at the other end of a relationship from the original entity class). The examples cited for both these situations involved single-valued attributes. However, the same applies to multi-valued attributes. Consider Figure 21, in which the value(s) of the **Meals** attribute are the same for a **Scheduled Flight** irrespective of **Departure Date**. This model is therefore not in 3rd Normal Form as it stands, but will be if the **Meals** attribute is moved to **Scheduled Flight**.

Figure 21: Meals on Flights (not in 3ʳᵈ Normal Form)

4.6   Multi-valued composite attributes

Multi-valued composite attributes are also possible. For example, a multi-currency **Account** could be modeled with a **Balances** attribute containing one or more sets of **Currency** and **Monetary Amount**. This can be depicted in a UML Class Diagram using a composite data type (**Monetary Amount** in this case) and an attribute (**Balance** in this case) marked with a **multiplicity**[39] of one or more. The multiplicities available in UML for attributes are the same as for relationships, discussed in Section 5.2. Here '1..*' means 'one or more'.

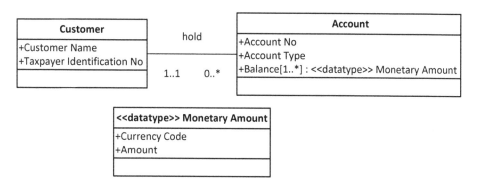

Figure 22: Multi-currency account in UML

---

[39] The **multiplicity** of an attribute is equivalent to the cardinality of a relationship, i.e., how many instances of the attribute may occur in one instance of the object class.

However, a multi-valued composite attribute is more difficult to depict in an Entity-Relationship Diagram. Again there are two options:

1. Create a **Monetary Amount** user-defined data type and document its components (**Currency Code** and **Amount**) in the free text metadata field provided by the tool to describe a domain. Associate the **Balances** attribute with that domain using its **attribute class** (see Section 4.7). As with all composite attributes, this adds to the conversion work when creating the logical data model from the business information model. However, it has the advantage that the business information model remains relatively simple (see Figure 23).

2. Create an **Account Balance** entity class in the business information model to represent all individual currency Balances and add a relationship between the **Account** entity class and the **Account Balance** entity class (see Figure 24). This makes the business information model rather more complex, and only simplifies creation of the logical data model from the business information model if the decision is taken to hold balances in a separate table. Bear in mind that multi-valued composite attributes are supported by many modern DBMSs (database management systems).

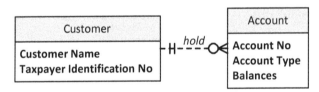

Figure 23: Multi-currency account with a multi-valued composite attribute

Again the relationship line between **Account** and the dependent entity class **Account Balance** is solid rather than dashed. This is to indicate that **Account** and **Account Balance** between them represent a single concept (**Account Balance** representing a multi-valued attribute of **Account**) rather than related concepts like **Customer** and **Account**. Again do not be concerned if your data modeling tool does not allow this distinction (which is useful but not essential).

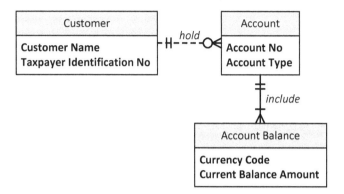

Figure 24: Multi-currency account as a separate dependent entity class

4.7   Attribute classes

It is clear from the attribute examples we've seen so far that some attributes are textual and some numeric. For this reason, many developers of conceptual data models fall for the temptation to give each attribute one of the **DBMS data types**[40] available in a database management system, such as **char(3)** or **integer**. This is inappropriate for two main reasons:

- Integers are used in databases for a variety of purposes. For example, in a school timetable database, integers may be used for:

    - timetable period numbers (e.g., Period 1, …, Period 8)
    - days of the week (e.g., 1 represents Monday, …, 5 represents Friday)
    - room capacities in terms of numbers of students that can be accommodated
    - numbers of active teaching periods per day per teacher.

---

[40] **DBMS data types** define the data that can be stored in a column of a table, in terms of valid values and allowed operations. Typical DBMS data types available are listed and described in Section 11.7.1.

- During conceptual data model development, the required maximum sizes of textual and numeric attributes are generally unknown and the DBMS may not have been selected.

DBMS data types are part of the *solution*. A business information model is a description of the *problem*.

Attribute classes (rather than DBMS data types) should be used in a business information model, with the following benefits:

- They provide a guide to giving attributes consistent, appropriate, and meaningful names (see Section 7.2).

- They support the creation and assignment of the appropriate **user-defined data types**[41] in the target DBMS (see Section 11.7.1).

- They enable the documentation of a richer picture of attribute properties and behavior, which supports verification of the business information model by the modeler and business stakeholders, and data access and manipulation code by developers.

The following sections enumerate the various types of **atomic attribute** (non-composite attribute).

4.7.1   Identifier attributes

A business information model should only include identifiers that will be visible to business users in the user interface or reports.

Data items included in a database design purely for integrity purposes should not be included in a business information model, but added to the corresponding logical data model (see Sections 11.6 and 11.8). These include

---

[41] All modern relational and object-relational DBMSs support user-defined data types.

non-visible **primary keys**[42] and *all* **foreign keys**[43]. The "every entity class requires a primary key" rule governing logical data models *does not* apply to business information models.

In fact, *any* candidate attribute that you are tempted to include which is not going to be visible in any user interface or report should not be included.

There are two types of visible identifiers:

- **natural identifiers** (or **business identifiers**) such as names of people, places, or things that have those names as a result of social processes and conventions generally external to the enterprise, e.g., **Customer Name**, **Locality Name**, **Country Name**

- **artificial identifiers** created by an external authority, such as a standards authority or registration authority (e.g., **Vehicle Registration No**, **Airport Code**, **Country Code**, **Taxpayer Identification No**), by a nominated authority within the enterprise (e.g., **Product Code**, **Flight No**), or automatically by a system (e.g., **Customer No**, **Order No**, **Account No**).

Note that identifier attributes in a business information model do not have to be **unique** (have a different value for every instance), unlike primary keys in a logical data model. In particular, natural identifiers such as customer names and locality names are often duplicated (have the same value for multiple instances) and need to be combined with other attributes to uniquely identify instances. For example, **Birth Date** is usually added to **Customer Name** to reduce (but not entirely eliminate) duplicates, and **State Code** is usually added to **Locality Name** for the same purpose.

---

[42] **Primary keys** are discussed in Section 11.6.
[43] **Foreign keys** are discussed in Section 11.8.1.

Each identifier attribute should be assigned an attribute class with the same name as the attribute.

4.7.2   Boolean attributes

Depending on business requirements, each **Boolean attribute** can either:

- only have the values True and False (often represented as Yes and No), to support **two-valued logic**[44], or

- only have the values True, False, and Unknown, to support **three-valued logic**[45].

Each Boolean attribute should be assigned the **Boolean** attribute class.

4.7.3   Set selection attributes

A **set selection attribute** (or **enumerated attribute**) is one that can only have values from a defined finite set, e.g., **Gender** (with values including Male, Female), **Travel Class** (with values including First, Business, Premium Economy, Economy), **Payment Method** (with values including Credit Card, Debit Card).

A separate attribute class is required for each such set of values, with the same name as the attribute minus any qualifying words. For example, if a **Passenger Reservation** entity class has **Initial Travel Class** and **Upgrade Travel Class** attributes, each of those attributes should use the attribute class **Travel Class**.

---

[44] **Two-valued logic** allows for a proposition to be only true or false.
[45] **Three-valued logic** is allows for a proposition to be true, false, or unknown.

4.7.4   Descriptor attributes

A **descriptor attribute** is one that describes an instance of a concept using text but is not generally used to identify it, e.g., **Product Description**, **Comment**.

Each descriptor attribute should be assigned the **Descriptor** attribute class.

4.7.5   Temporal attributes

A **temporal attribute** is one that records when some event has happened or is to happen. There are two types of temporal attributes:

- A **single point-in-time attribute** records when a single event has happened or is to happen. The attribute classes for this type of attribute are:
    - **Datetime**, for attributes that record a date and time of day, e.g., **Equipment Return Date and Time**
    - **Date**, for attributes that record a complete date (year, month, day), e.g., **Birth Date** of a **Customer**, **Order Date**
    - **Year No**, for attributes that record just a year, e.g., **Model Year** of a **Road Vehicle**.

- A **recurrent point-in-time attribute** records when a recurrent event happens. The attribute classes for this type of attribute are:
    - **Day of Week**, for attributes that record the day of the week on which a weekly event occurs, e.g., **Late Closing Day**
    - **Time of Day**, for attributes that record a time of day, e.g., **Flight Departure Time**
    - **Time of Week**, for attributes that record a day of week and time of day, e.g., **Weekly Meeting Time**
    - **Day of Week of Month**, for attributes that record an ordinal (1st, 2nd, 3rd, 4th, last) and day of week, e.g., monthly **Timesheet Submission Day**
    - **Time of Week of Month**, for attributes that record an ordinal (1st, 2nd, 3rd, 4th, last), day of week and time of day, e.g., **Start Time** of a monthly **Meeting**

- ○ **Day of Month**, for attributes that record a day of month (from 1 to 31), e.g., monthly **Mortgage Repayment Date**
- ○ **Day of Year**, for attributes that record a month and a day (but no year), e.g., **Annual Fee Deduction Date**.

Each temporal attribute should be assigned the appropriate attribute class from the list above.

With any temporal attribute involving time of day the following questions need to be asked:

- Do times in different time zones need to be considered?
- Does daylight saving ("summer time") need to be taken into account?

Generally speaking, time zones need to be considered by any enterprise whose operations, customers, and/or suppliers are in more than one time zone.

Daylight saving is generally only an issue for:

- enterprises with operations, customers, and/or suppliers in more than one jurisdiction where:
  - ○ some of those jurisdictions observe daylight saving while others do not (e.g., States in the US and Australia), or
  - ○ those jurisdictions may change to or from daylight saving on different dates (e.g., States in Australia), or
- enterprises with overnight processes which may traverse a change to or from daylight saving (e.g., overnight flights or train schedules).

4.7.6   Quantifier attributes

A **quantifier attribute** is any attribute that records some quantifiable property of an instance of a concept. There are two types of quantifier attributes:

1. A **dimensioned quantifier attribute** requires a unit of measure to be meaningful, e.g.,

   - **Transaction Amount**, measured in a specific currency
   - **Flight Leg Distance**, measured in miles in the US and Km elsewhere
   - **Vehicle Weight**, measured in pounds in the US and Kg elsewhere
   - **Trip Duration**, usually measured in minutes
   - **Maximum Speed**, measured in mph in the US and Km/h elsewhere.

2. A **dimensionless quantifier attribute** does not require a unit of measure to be meaningful. There are three types of dimensionless quantifier attributes:

   - A **count** (or **cardinal number**) records how many of some object of interest there are in a particular context, e.g., **Number of Standing Passengers**. The attribute class **Count** should be used for this type of attribute.
   - A **sequence number** (or **ordinal number**) records the place of some object within a sequence, e.g., **Emergency Contact Sequence**. The attribute class **Ordinal** should be used for this type of attribute.
   - A **ratio**, **rate**, or **factor** (usually represented as a percentage) records the proportion of some quantity with respect to some other quantity, e.g., **Exchange Rate**, **Blood Alcohol Concentration**. The attribute class **Factor** should be used only when comparing two dimensionless quantifier attributes, or two dimensioned quantifier attributes with the same dimension, e.g., two lengths, areas, volumes, weights, durations, or monetary amounts. It cannot be used for comparisons of dimensioned quantifier attributes with different dimensions, for which there are specific dimensioned quantifier attribute classes (see above). For example, speed is a ratio of distance and time, density is a ratio of weight and volume.

There are many potential dimensioned quantifier attribute classes, one for every base unit and derived unit in the **International System of Units** (also known by its French initials **SI**) but those most likely to be found in an application system are:

- **Duration**, **Interval**
- **Length**, **Area**, **Volume**
- **Mass**, **Weight**
- **Temperature**
- **Voltage**, **Frequency**, **Electric Current**, **Resistance**, **Power**, **Energy**, **Charge**
- **Speed**, **Acceleration**
- **Density**.

I recommend that each dimensioned quantifier attribute be constrained to use a single unit of measure, but some business environments require the ability to record values with different units of measure, e.g., different currencies or a mix of pounds and Kg. If this is genuinely the case, a composite attribute must be used, consisting of a quantifier component and a set selection component, e.g., a composite **Transaction Amount** attribute consisting of a **Monetary Amount** and a **Currency**, or a composite **Product Weight** attribute consisting of a **Weight** and a **Weight Unit**.

4.7.7   Media attributes

There is a growing trend for enterprises to use media, such as:

- images (e.g., **Identity Card Photograph**, **Station Map**)
- sound recordings (e.g., **Emergency Call Recording**)
- video recordings (e.g., **CCTV Recording**).

If such attributes are required, they should use attribute class **Image**, **Sound Recording**, or **Video Recording** as appropriate.

4.7.8   Documenting simple attribute classes

Most Entity-Relationship modeling tools support the use of simple attribute classes and most (if not all) refer to them as **domains**.

If you are using a UML tool, each simple attribute class can be documented as a **user-defined data type**[46].

4.7.9   Attribute class operations

Most versions of SQL allow any two numeric data items to be compared, added, subtracted, multiplied, or divided. However, as I illustrated at the start of Section 4.7, there are many different classes of numeric data types. Most are limited in terms of the operations in which they can legitimately participate. Process design for a new application system based on the business information model can (and should) use this knowledge to verify the appropriateness of proposed data manipulation.

4.7.9.1   Comparisons

Attributes of *the same* attribute class *can* legitimately be compared using the =, ≠, <, >, ≤, ≥, and between operators, whereas attributes of *different* attribute classes *cannot*, e.g., neither **Order No** = **Product Code** nor **Customer No** = **Quantity Ordered** makes sense.

Only *identifier* or *descriptor* attributes can be compared using the like operator, e.g., where **Product Code** like 'LP%', where **Product Name** like '%Turntable%'.

---

[46] **Data types** define the data that can be stored in a column of a table, in terms of valid values and allowed operations. Each DBMS provides a number of built-in data types, a representative sample of which are listed and described in Section 11.7.1. Many DBMSs allow users to define **user-defined data types** based on built-in data types.

4.7.9.2 Arithmetic operations

Dimensioned quantifier attributes of the same attribute class *can* legitimately be added or subtracted, the result being of the same attribute class, e.g., **Tare Weight + Net Weight**.

Counts *can* legitimately be added or subtracted, the result being a count, e.g., **Quantity Ordered – Quantity Delivered**.

Two sequence numbers *cannot* legitimately be added but can legitimately be subtracted, e.g., when comparing positions in a queue.

Two ratios, rates, or factors *can* legitimately be multiplied or divided and *may* with care be added or subtracted, e.g., **Standard Discount Rate + Special Discount Rate**.

In general, a duration *can* be legitimately added to or subtracted from a temporal attribute, the result being of the same class as the temporal attribute, e.g., **Departure Time + Trip Duration**.

Two single point-in-time attributes of the same attribute class *can* legitimately be subtracted, the result being a duration, but *cannot* legitimately be added, e.g., **Departure Time – Arrival Time**.

Two quantifier attributes can legitimately be multiplied or divided *only* in certain combinations. For example:

- any quantifier attribute can be multiplied or divided by a count, ratio, rate, or factor, e.g., **Unit Price × Quantity Ordered**
- some quantifier attributes can be divided by a duration, e.g., **Trip Distance / Trip Duration**
- some dimensioned quantifier attributes of the same class can be divided, e.g., **Package Weight / Unit Weight**

- some dimensioned quantifier attributes of different classes can be multiplied or divided, e.g., **Weight** / **Volume**.

4.8   Summary

The instances of each entity class of interest to the enterprise are identified and/or described using attributes.

We should (a) exercise judgment in deciding what attributes to include in the model, (b) include only those attributes we would expect to see represented in a user interface or web page maintained by the enterprise, and (c) not make assumptions about what attributes the enterprise is interested in.

In a business information model, normalization (assigning attributes to the right entity classes) is important. An attribute should be assigned to a different entity class if the answers are Yes to both of the following questions:

- Does this attribute always have the same value when some other attribute has the same value?

- Can that other attribute have the same value in multiple instances of this entity class?

Assigning an attribute to a particular entity class can support functionality such as providing for different delivery dates or delivery addresses for different items in an order.

Derived attributes should be included if they are of business importance.

Composite and multi-valued attributes can be useful ways of representing complex information requirements simply, provided your modeling tool supports their use. Entity-Relationship modeling tools and UML tools provide different ways of modeling attributes.

Multi-valued attributes appear to violate 1st Normal Form. However, 1st Normal Form is not required in a business information model, not necessarily required in a logical data model, and not a prerequisite for a model to be in higher normal forms such as 3rd Normal Form.

Attribute classes (a) help to ensure attributes are given consistent appropriate meaningful names, (b) support the creation and assignment of the appropriate data types in the target DBMS, and (c) support verification of data access and manipulation code.

Chapter 5.   Relationships between concepts

In the models that have appeared in previous chapters, various **relationships** between concepts have been depicted. For example, in Figure 25, the following relationships are depicted:

- **Customer** *holds* **Account** (alternatively worded as **Account** *is held by* **Customer**)

- **Account** *includes* **Account Balance** (**Account Balance** *is included in* **Account**).

5.1   Documenting relationships

If you are using an Entity-Relationship modeling tool, each relationship should be documented as a **relationship** between the relevant **entity classes** (or **entities**). If you are using a UML tool, each relationship should be documented as an **association** between the relevant **object classes**. Let's revisit the multi-currency account model from the previous chapter:

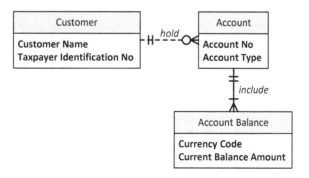

Figure 25: Multi-currency account (revisited)

5.2   Cardinality and optionality

Each end of a relationship has two properties:

The **cardinality** of a relationship end defines how many instances of the adjacent entity class may be associated *at any given time* with one instance of the opposite entity class. In Entity-Relationship Diagrams, the cardinality may be (a) limited to one only (indicated by a crossbar), or (b) allowed to be more than one (indicated by a "crow's foot"). Thus, in the relationship in Figure 25 between **Customer** and **Account**,

- one Customer can hold one or more Accounts
- one Account can only be held by one Customer.

The **optionality** of a relationship end defines whether an instance of the opposite entity class may exist at any time without an associated instance of the adjacent entity class. In Entity-Relationship Diagrams, the optionality may be mandatory (indicated by a crossbar), or optional (indicated by a circle). Thus in the relationship in Figure 25 between **Customer** and **Account**,

- a Customer can exist without an associated Account
- an Account cannot exist without an associated Customer.

Think of the circle, crossbar, and "crow's foot" symbols as representing 0, 1, and ≥ 0[47] respectively.

In **UML Class Diagrams**, these properties are conflated. Each relationship end is marked with the minimum and maximum numbers of instances of the adjacent object class that can be associated with an instance of the opposite object class.

---

[47] ≥ 0 means 0, 1, or more.

'0..*' represents ≥0 whereas '1..*' represents ≥1. The model in Figure 26 is equivalent to that in Figure 25.

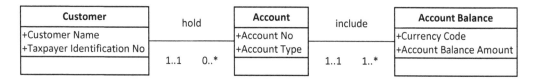

Figure 26: Associations in a UML class model

In UML generally, values other than 0, 1, and ≥1 can be represented. For example, if there is a business-imposed limit of ten Order Items per Order, the '1..*' symbol in Figure 26 would be replaced by '1..10'. However, this is not supported by all tools.

All but one of the relationships in the models that have appeared so far in this book have been "one to many" with cardinality 1 at one end and ≥0 at the other. The only exceptions so far have been the "one to one" relationships with cardinality 1 at each end in Figure 5 in Section 3.1.

Be careful using the term "one to many". I once asked a business stakeholder whether an Order could be raised for goods destined for many Departments. His reply was "No, only ever one or two". Other, better labels for such relationships are "one to zero or more", "1:≥0", and "1:n". I prefer "1:n" and will use it henceforth.

5.3   When not to use a 1:n relationship

Most systems include attributes whose values are drawn from discrete finite **enumerated sets** (often referred to as **domains** in line with the definition of that term in mathematics). For example, in Figure 27, **Pay Grade**, **Employment Status**, and **Leave Type** are all enumerated sets:

- **Employment Status** might have the values Permanent and Temporary

- **Leave Type** might have the values Sick Leave, Annual Leave, Jury Service, and Compassionate Leave.

Many data modelers depict each such classification as a "**type table**" and a relationship to the entity class being classified, as in Figure 27. This *may* be appropriate in the logical data model *if* there is a consensus within the development team that that is the appropriate way to implement classification schemes, but there are other ways to implement them.

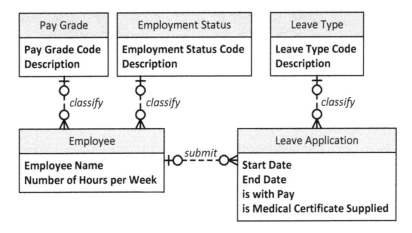

Figure 27: Employee Leave Applications (not recommended as a business information model)

In a business information model, it is inappropriate to include implementation detail. We should instead model this scenario as in Figure 28. It is much simpler and easier to comprehend—and hence review—yet includes the same information as Figure 27 except the fact that **Pay Grade**, **Employment Status**, and **Leave Type** are enumerated sets.

As we saw in Section 4.7, each enumerated set attribute should be marked as a **set selection attribute** by way of its **attribute class**. Unless your data modeling tool can display attribute classes in diagrams, they should be recorded in the accompanying documentation. Remember, *no diagram should ever be reviewed without reading the accompanying documentation.*

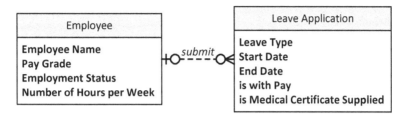

Figure 28: Employee Leave Application business information model

5.4 n:n relationships

There are also "many to many" (or "n:n" relationships). For example, most large businesses involved in the travel and accommodation sector record which languages their customer-facing employees speak fluently, so that the appropriate flags can be displayed on their name badges[48]. There are Employees who speak more than one Language and Languages spoken by more than one Employee. This is illustrated in Figure 29, which also identifies each Guest's preferred Language, enabling the accommodation provider to handle interactions with Guests proactively.

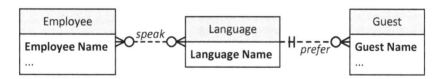

Figure 29: An n:n relationship

By the way, note the use of the ellipsis symbol ('…') which is an indication that there are other **Employee** and **Guest** attributes not shown (either because we

---

[48] Quite how this works in practice I'm not sure, as there is an n:n relationship between Countries and their official Languages. For example, what flag would be displayed if an employee speaks Mandarin but not Cantonese or *vice versa*?

haven't analyzed them yet or to keep the diagram uncluttered). Not every tool allows you to do this.

5.4.1   n:n relationship or multi-valued attribute?

Figure 30 is a fragment of a model of an IT consultancy practice, which assigns consultants to projects based on their competencies. The **Competency** entity class would have instances for each DBMS, methodology, development tool, and so on. A business information model could alternatively represent this n:n relationship as a multi-valued attribute, as in Figure 31, but *only* if (a) no attributes other than the Name of each Competency are required, *and* (b) there is no requirement for additional information about each Competency of each Consultant.

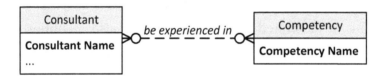

Figure 30: A consultancy practice

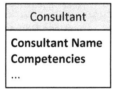

Figure 31: A multi-valued attribute rather than an n:n relationship

Note that the multi-valued attribute is named **Competencies** rather than **Competency Names**. This is to align more closely with what the business stakeholders would expect the user interface to display. Naming of attributes is discussed in detail in Section 7.2.

5.4.2   n:n relationship or time-variant 1:n relationship?

Graeme Simsion and I were once criticized by an apparently experienced data modeler for having used a 1:n relationship rather than an n:n relationship in one of the examples in *Data Modeling Essentials* (see Figure 32).

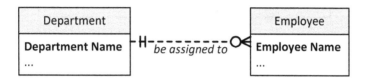

Figure 32: Assignment of Employees to Departments

His reasoning was that an Employee may be assigned to more than one Department over time, so the relationship in this example should be n:n. While it is true that reassignment can occur ***over time***, it is standard practice to model the relationships that can exist ***at a point in time***, at least in the model to be shared with business stakeholders for review.

If a record of previous assignments is required in the system being modeled, the more complex data structures required to support this should be included in the ***logical data model***[49]. Including them in the business information model is likely to compromise the effectiveness of its review by business stakeholders. Remember, *the more complex a model is, the more likely anyone reviewing the model will fail to notice an issue with the model*.

If proof were needed of the semantic difference between an n:n relationship and a time-variant 1:n relationship, it was provided when I had to resolve some problems with a system that produced regional statistics that "didn't add up".

---

[49] This is discussed in Section 11.12.

At any given time, a Local Government Area (LGA) is in one and only one Region, as depicted in Figure 33.

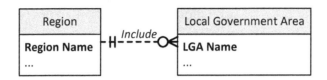

Figure 33: Allocation of LGAs to Regions

However, every so often, the Regions are reorganized, meaning that one or more LGAs are each reallocated to a different Region. The application system had been developed using Hibernate, which apparently automatically creates a database structure from the user interface design. The developers knew that LGAs could be reallocated to different Regions, and knew just enough data modeling to decide that an n:n relationship would support this, so they coded accordingly. They completely overlooked the fact that at any given time a LGA is in one and only one Region, and didn't include any controls to prevent a LGA from being simultaneously allocated to more than one Region.

The inevitable happened and, during the first reorganization, a user allocated a LGA to a new Region without removing it from its previous Region. Within days the statistics weren't adding up.

5.5   1:1 relationships

These are less common than 1:n or n:n relationships. However, 1:1 relationships that are mandatory at one end and optional at the other can relate a concept to roles played by that concept (as in Figure 5 in Section 3.1). Those that are optional at both ends occur occasionally, whereas those that are mandatory at both ends are rarely seen.

5.6   Recording changes in time-variant data

The anecdote in Section 5.4.2 illustrates how important it is to properly handle changing data in a database. Actually, it is not so much the possibility of data changing that complicates matters as the requirement to keep a record of changes over time. If the enterprise only needs to record the current state of each entity class and relationship, no additional data structures and processing are required to record historical states. If, however, there is a requirement to record historical states, additional data structures and processing are required.

However, as I stated in the previous discussion, any such additional data structures should *not* be included in the business information model, as the extra complexity is likely to compromise the effectiveness of review of the model by business stakeholders.

Despite this, the requirement for recording history should be identified during the development of the business information model. This requirement may be explicitly stated, but may also arise from reporting requirements, in particular year on year or other time-variant statistics. If there are requirements for time-variant statistics, history must be recorded for (a) the quantities to be compared, (b) any other quantities with which they should be compared, and (c) the categories by which those quantities are to be distinguished.

For example, if there is a requirement to compare deaths per head of population from various causes among persons in various occupations in various states month by month, the following need to be recorded for each month:

- the number of deaths in each state broken down by cause and occupation
- the mean population of each state in each month
- the number of persons in each occupation in each state during each month.

Having established a requirement for recording history, there are various possible approaches:

- Record this requirement in a document separate from the model.

- If your data modeling tool provides a specific metadata field in which to document whether history is required and that field allows the values Yes, No, and Unknown, use that field to mark those entity classes, attributes, and relationships appropriately.

- Alternatively, append "history required" or "history not required" (as appropriate) to the contents of the definition field for each entity class, attribute, and relationship. If there is data for which you don't yet know whether history is required, the absence of any reference to history indicates that the requirement needs to be established before the logical data model can be developed.

- If your data modeling tool provides the option to add text or graphics to the data model diagram, I have found that the symbols ☺ and ☐ provide an intuitive visual metaphor for "history required" and "history not required" respectively. Again, the absence of either symbol indicates that the requirement has not yet been established.

Where there is a requirement for recording history, any additional data structures should be added during the development of the logical data model, as described in Section 11.12.

5.7   Recursive relationships

There can be relationships between instances of the same entity class. For example, all but one Employee reports to one other Employee, and there are Employees who manage a number of other Employees, as depicted in Figure 34.

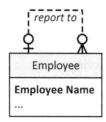

Figure 34: A recursive relationship

Note that this relationship represents a **hierarchy**[50] (as do most 1:n recursive relationships). Relationships representing hierarchies must be *optional at both ends*: in this case, there must be an Employee who does not report to another Employee and there are many Employees who do not manage other Employees. If a relationship representing a hierarchy were mandatory at either end, that hierarchy would have to have an infinite number of levels, which would be beyond the capacity of any DBMS.

Recursive n:n relationships also exist. For example, many Countries border other Countries, and many of them have borders with more than one other Country, as depicted in Figure 35.

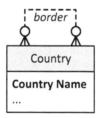

Figure 35: A recursive n:n relationship

---

[50] A **hierarchy** is an arrangement of persons, organizations, things, or concepts represented as being above, below, or at the same level as one another.

Beware! Sometimes a relationship appears to be a recursive n:n relationship but is the result of a simpler phenomenon. A student administration system may well need to record a student's siblings, typically because a fee discount may be offered to the second and subsequent students in a family. It's tempting to model this as a recursive n:n relationship on the **Student** entity class, but the number of instances of that relationship would grow at an increasing rate as each child in a family enrolls. For example, when the fifth child in a family enrolls, that new student must be associated with each of their older siblings. That would either present a data entry nightmare or require program code to propagate the sibling relationship across all pairs in a family once a new student was identified as a sibling of an existing student.

Once we think about this scenario in those terms, a simpler model becomes apparent. An optional 1:n recursive relationship on the **Student** entity class can be used to relate that Student to one of their older siblings (if any). For consistency, this should be either the oldest or the youngest in each case, the youngest if a student record is deleted after that Student leaves, or the oldest if records are retained. This is illustrated in Figure 36.

Now that we're looking at alternatives and, I hope, asking the question "what are we really modeling here?" we may realize that it would be possible to derive this relationship from information about each student's parents (assuming that is also in the model). This, in turn, raises questions about how the term **Sibling** is defined:

- another student who has the same biological parents as the student in question?

- another student who has at least one biological parent the same as the student in question?

- another student who lives with the same adult (or adults) as the student in question?

This is an example of an important fact: *developing a business information model raises questions about the policies and rules governing how the enterprise does business.*

5.8   Derived relationships

We have just established that we can derive the existence of a student's older sibling from knowledge of the parents or guardians of each student. If your data modeling tool allows non-alphabetic characters in relationship names, agree with the business stakeholders what character to use as a prefix or suffix in the name of each derived relationship. As with attributes, one candidate is the oblique ('/') which is used in UML class models to mark derived relationships as well as attributes, as in Figure 36. Be sure to use the same prefix or suffix for both derived attributes and derived relationships.

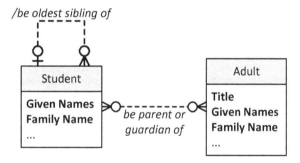

Figure 36: A derived relationship

5.9   Attributes of relationships

Consider Figure 37. In this model, an **Employee** may be certified in one or more **Competencies** and more than one **Employee** may be certified in the same **Competency**.

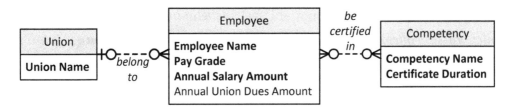

Figure 37: Attributes of relationships

The certificate for each Competency is only valid for a limited period, after which an Employee must be recertified if they are to continue to exercise that competency. Clearly, we need an attribute to represent the date on which each Employee was last certified for each relevant Competency.

Such an attribute cannot be an attribute of **Employee**, since any Employee with more than one Competency will have more than one certification date. Similarly it cannot be an attribute of **Competency**, since any Competency in which more than one Employee is certified will have more than one certification date. Remember one of the key questions to ask is, "Can this attribute have more than one value at the same time for this concept?"

In fact, **Certification Date** is an attribute of the relationship between **Employee** and **Competency**. Similarly, an **Employee** may belong to a **Union** but is not obliged to. The **Annual Union Dues Amount** attribute is actually an attribute of the relationship between **Employee** and **Union**. It is optional but must be present for each **Employee** that belongs to a **Union** and absent for each **Employee** that does not belong to a **Union**.

5.9.1 Documenting attributes of relationships

How can we show these as attributes of relationships in the diagram? If we use a **UML Class Diagram** to depict our model, we can use an **association class**[51] to hold attributes of relationships, as in Figure 38.

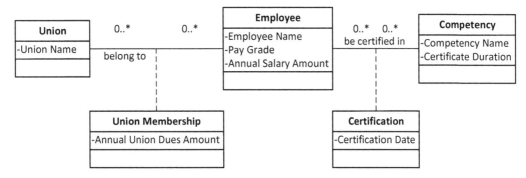

Figure 38: Attributes of relationships in a UML Class Diagram

This notation isn't available in the Entity-Relationship Diagrams we've been using up to now, so we have to use an entity class box to represent **Certification** details, as in Figure 39. Note that:

- the relationship between **Employee** and **Competency**, which was an **n:n relationship** in Figure 37, has been replaced by an **intersection entity class**[52] and two **1:n relationships**

- the cardinality of each of the new 1:n relationships is 'optional 1 or more'[53] of the new entity class and '1' of the original entity class. In this case, each **Employee** may have one or more **Certifications**, and each

---

[51] An **association class** is an **association** (the UML equivalent of a **relationship**) represented using an **object class** (the UML equivalent of an **entity class**).

[52] An **intersection entity class** is an **n:n relationship** (see Section 5.4) represented using an **entity class**.

[53] This is often expressed as "zero or more", but I advise against doing so in Section 7.3.

Competency may be the subject of one or more **Certifications**, but each **Certification** is for one **Employee** and one **Competency**.

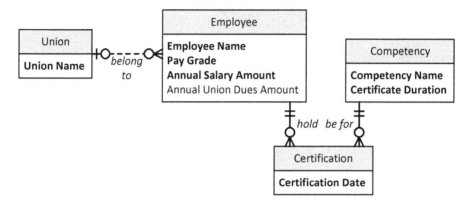

Figure 39: Attribute of an n:n relationship in an intersection entity class

The new relationship lines are solid rather than dashed. This is to indicate that the intersection entity class and its relationships represent a single concept (the n:n relationship between **Employee** and **Competency**). Again, do not be concerned if your data modeling tool does not allow this distinction (which is useful but not essential).

5.10   Summary

All data modeling tools provide a means of documenting relationships between concepts. All tools allow you to mark each end to indicate (a) whether more than one instance of the adjacent entity class can be associated *at any given time* with one instance of the opposite entity class, and (b) whether there must always be at least one instance of the adjacent entity class for each instance of the opposite entity class.

If an attribute has values drawn from an enumerated set (or domain), it should not be represented in a business information model as a relationship to a "type table", as that is an implementation detail.

While most relationships are 1:n, there are also 1:1 and n:n relationships.

Time-variant 1:n relationships for which history is required should not be represented as n:n relationships.

A multi-valued attribute can sometimes be used instead of an n:n relationship to produce a simpler model.

A recursive relationship relates instances of the same entity class to each other, as in a hierarchy, although there are relationships other than hierarchies which are recursive.

Relationships can be derived from other information.

Relationships may have attributes.

Chapter 6.   Generalization and specialization

Some concepts are broad, in that they embrace many instances (actually or potentially), while others are relatively narrow. Consider **Road Vehicle**, **Automobile**, **Bus**, and **Truck**. Automobiles, Buses, and Trucks are all Road Vehicles but not all Road Vehicles are Trucks. Once we become aware of the possibility of specializing the concept **Road Vehicle**, all sorts of questions arise:

- Assuming the enterprise needs to manage information about Road Vehicles, what types of Road Vehicle is it interested in (and why)? The answer will depend on the type of enterprise: a vehicle registration authority, an insurance company offering vehicle insurance, and an enterprise operating a fleet of vehicles could well have different information requirements.

- Is the enterprise likely to have different information requirements for different types of Road Vehicles? For example, the number of seats in each Automobile and the number of seated and standing passengers in each Bus would be of interest, whereas the maximum loaded weight of each Truck would be of interest. However, other information requirements apply to all Road Vehicles, such as registration number, registration expiry date, and engine capacity.

- If the enterprise is also interested in non-powered Road Vehicles, such as Trailers,

    o   is it interested in non-powered Road Vehicles other than Trailers?

> o   is it interested in different types of Trailers, such as caravans (mobile homes), boat trailers, and semi-trailers?
> o   non-powered Road Vehicles do not have engines, so engine capacity is irrelevant.

- A Utility Vehicle (or Pickup) is a cross between an Automobile and a Truck.

- Is the enterprise also interested in Vans, Motorcycles, or Mobile Homes? If so, do these have different data requirements?

Here we're starting to develop a **taxonomy**[54] of concepts, tailored to suit the enterprise. When modeling a taxonomy, we refer to the more specialized concepts as **subtypes** and the more generalized concept as the **supertype**[55].

6.1   Subtypes with different attributes

Before we actually develop the model we need to itemize the attributes that are required, and establish which attributes apply to which types of Road Vehicle. The following attributes are likely to be useful:

- Registration details (these apply to all types of **Road Vehicle**):

  - o   **Registration No**
  - o   **Registration State Code**
  - o   **Registration Expiry Date**

---

[54] A **taxonomy** is a collection of concepts and the terms that signify those concepts, each with a definition. Except for a small set of top-level concepts, each concept is recorded as being a specialized variety of some more general concept. For example, Businesses, Government Bodies, and Not-for-Profit Organizations are each particular types of Organization.

[55] A **subtype** is an **entity class** that contains some (but not all) of the members of some other entity class (its **supertype**) but no instances that are not members of the supertype. For example, the entity class **Wide-Body Aircraft** is a subtype of the entity class **Aircraft** (all Wide-Body Aircraft are Aircraft but not all Aircraft are Wide-Body Aircraft).

- Description:

  - **Make**: this applies to all types of **Road Vehicle**
  - **Model**: this applies to all types of **Road Vehicle**
  - **Model Year**: this applies to all types of **Road Vehicle**
  - **Propulsion Type** (Petrol, Diesel, Hybrid, Electric, Hydrogen): this applies to all types of **Road Vehicle** except **Trailers**
  - **Engine Capacity**: this applies to all types of **Road Vehicle** except **Trailers** and those with some **Propulsion Types**
  - **Body Type**: this applies to all types of **Road Vehicle** except **Buses**
  - **Number of Seats**: this applies to all types of **Road Vehicle** except **Trucks** and **Trailers**
  - **Number of Standing Passengers**: this applies only to **Buses**
  - **Maximum Loaded Weight**: this applies only to **Utility Vehicles, Trucks, and Trailers**[56]
  - **Tare Weight**: this also applies only to **Utility Vehicles, Trucks, and Trailers**
  - **Number of Axles**: this applies to all types of **Road Vehicle** except **Automobiles**

- Ownership details:

  - **Owner Name**: this applies to all types of **Road Vehicle**
  - **Lessee Name**: this *may* apply to any type of **Road Vehicle**.[57]

How should we model this?

One possibility is as illustrated in Figure 40, in which any attribute that (a) applies to all types of **Road Vehicle** (e.g., **Registration No** but not **Tare Weight**) and

---

[56] In fact, **Maximum Loaded Weight, Tare Weight**, and **Number of Axles** apply to all types of **Road Vehicle** but are typically not recorded for the other vehicle types.

[57] Note the distinction: every registered **Road Vehicle** has an Owner but not every **Road Vehicle** is leased.

(b) applies to all **Road Vehicles** (e.g., **Owner Name** but not **Lessee Name**) are mandatory, all others being optional.

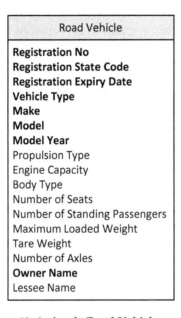

Figure 40: A simple Road Vehicle concept

This model suffers from two drawbacks:

1. It is not clear which attributes apply to which types of Road Vehicle. We have taken the trouble to find out but have then not documented this in the model. There are, of course, other ways of documenting this:

    o   in the attribute definitions (see Section 7.5.2)
    o   using **data rules** (see Chapter 8), although these are often deferred until the logical data model is developed rather than included in the business information model.

2. There is no distinction between attributes that apply only to some types of Road Vehicle (e.g., **Maximum Loaded Weight**) and those that apply to all types of Road Vehicle but not all individual Road Vehicles (e.g., **Lessee Name**).

An alternative is illustrated in Figure 41, in which (a) all attributes that apply to all types of Road Vehicle are retained in the **Road Vehicle** entity class, and (b) each attribute that applies only to some types of Road Vehicle is assigned to each of the **subtypes** representing those types of Road Vehicle.

A further alternative is illustrated in Figure 42, in which those attributes that apply to all types of Road Vehicle except **Trailers** are separated into the intermediate subtype **Powered Road Vehicle**. This avoids the repetition of **Propulsion Type** and **Engine Capacity**.

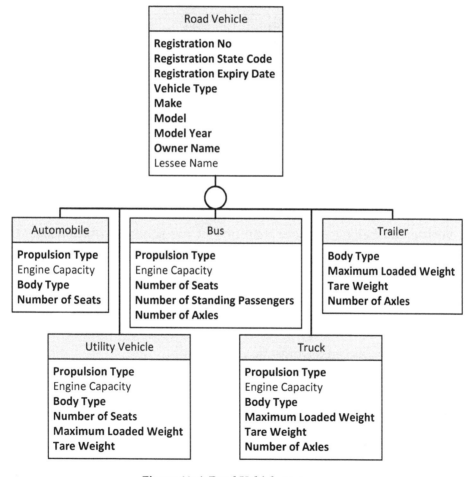

Figure 41: A Road Vehicle taxonomy

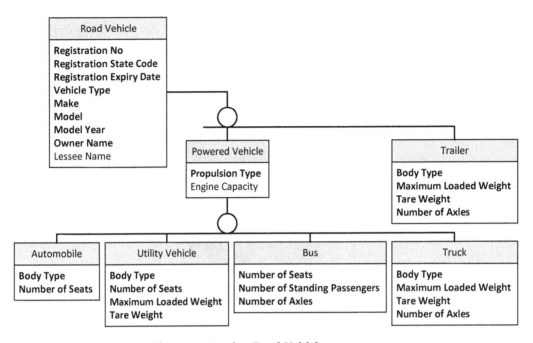

Figure 42: Another Road Vehicle taxonomy

6.2   Mutually exclusive taxonomies

The taxonomies above are all **mutually exclusive**, meaning that no individual **Road Vehicle** can belong to more than one of the subtypes (**Automobile**, **Utility Vehicle**, **Bus**, **Truck**, and **Trailer** in Figure 41). However, taxonomies can be **overlapping** (not mutually exclusive). For example, **Customers** may be subtyped as **Overseas Customer**, **Domestic Customer**, **Business Customer**, and **Personal Customer**. Clearly, an Overseas Customer can be either a Business Customer or a Personal Customer, as can a Domestic Customer.

6.3   Jointly exhaustive taxonomies

A taxonomy is **jointly exhaustive** if each instance of the **supertype** (in this case, **Road Vehicle**) belongs to at least one subtype. Thus the taxonomy in Figure 41 is only jointly exhaustive if no road vehicles other than automobiles, utility vehicles, buses, trucks, and trailers are of interest to the enterprise.

6.4   Subtypes with different relationships

In Section 3.1, we modeled the roles that may be played by a **Party** (**Customer**, **Supplier**, and **Employee**) and noted that only **Persons** can play the **Employee** role, whereas both **Persons** and **Organizations** can play the **Customer** and **Supplier** roles. The model depicted in that section (reproduced here as Figure 43) did not document that constraint.

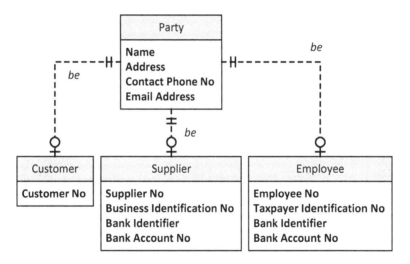

Figure 43: Roles played by Parties

Now that we have subtypes in our toolbox, we can use them to document that constraint, as illustrated in Figure 44. **Employee** is related to **Person** (but not to **Organization**), whereas **Customer** and **Supplier** are each related to **Party**, which embraces both **Person** and **Organization**.

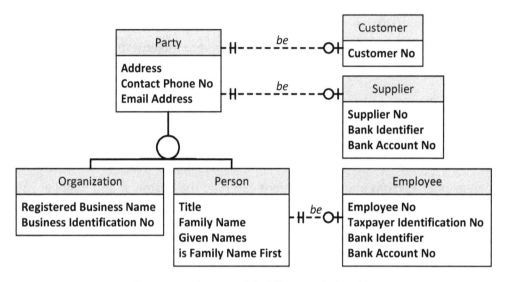

Figure 44: Subtypes with different relationships

6.5   Documenting subtypes in a data modeling tool

If you are using an Entity-Relationship modeling tool, each set of subtypes should be documented as **subtypes** of the **entity class** representing the relevant supertype.

If you are using a UML tool, each set of subtypes should be documented as **subclasses** of the **object class** representing the relevant supertype.

6.6   Attribute generalization

There are three ways in which attributes may possibly be generalized:

- generalization of similar attributes across a set of role entity classes
- generalization of similar attributes across the subtypes of a supertype
- generalization of similar attributes of the one entity class.

6.6.1 Attribute generalization across role entity classes

Recall the model in Figure 43.

There are some similar attributes in the role entity classes **Customer**, **Supplier**, and **Employee**:

- **Customer No**, **Supplier No**, and **Employee No**
- **Bank Identifier** in **Supplier** and **Employee**
- **Bank Account No** in **Supplier** and **Employee**.

It is almost an "article of faith" in the data modeling community that generalization is a good thing, so why don't we generalize each of these sets of similar attributes, to produce the model in Figure 45?

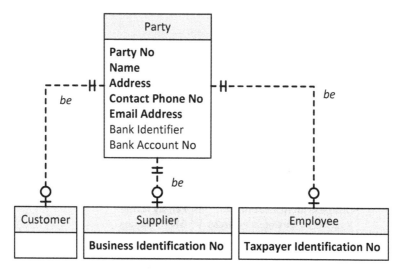

Figure 45: Over-generalized attributes (not recommended)

There are two problems with this model:

1. Whereas in Figure 43 we documented that Bank Identifiers and Bank Account Nos are mandatory for both Suppliers and Employees, moving the **Bank Identifier** and **Bank Account No** attributes into **Party** loses that

constraint: this model allows a Supplier or Employee to be recorded without bank account details.

2. The terms **Customer No**, **Supplier No**, and **Employee No** would be understood by business stakeholders whereas they would most likely be unfamiliar with the term **Party No**.

Since there is no particular advantage in making these changes, I do not recommend them.

6.6.2   Attribute generalization across subtypes

Many enterprises have both customers who are individual Persons and customers who are Organizations, such as other enterprises. Persons and Organizations have different but similar attributes, as illustrated in Figure 46.

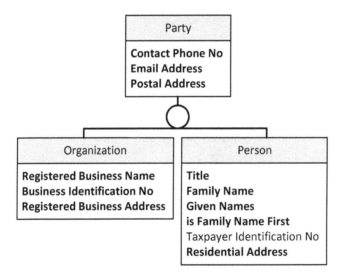

Figure 46: Party subtypes

There appears to be some scope for generalizing attributes:

*   **Registered Business Address** and **Residential Address** could be combined into a single **Address** attribute in the **Party** entity class, but there would then be the possibility of confusion between **Address** and **Postal Address**.

Note that the terms Registered Business Address and Residential Address have specific legal meanings (at least in Australia).

- **Business Identification No** and **Taxpayer Identification No**[58] could possibly be combined into a single **Party** attribute, but what name could it be given?

- If the **Title**, **Family Name**, **Given Names** and **is Family Name First** attributes of **Person** were replaced by a single **Name** attribute, it could be combined with **Registered Business Name** into a single **Party Name** attribute in the **Party** entity class, but with a significant loss of semantic precision.

In short, unless two attributes in different subtypes have the same meaning and the same name (or you can concoct a name that business stakeholders understand and that accurately signifies both attributes), leave them in the subtypes. Note the **is Family Name First** attribute in the **Person** entity class, and the use of **Family Name** and **Given Names** rather than **First Name** and **Last Name**. This is the correct way to model person names in any culturally diverse organization or customer base, as there are many cultures (e.g., East Asian, Eastern European) in which the family name precedes the given names. Any system that requests a customer to provide their First Name and Last Name risks the enterprise having no idea which of those names is the customer's family name.

6.6.3   Attribute generalization within an entity class

Consider Figure 47, which depicts the publishing schedule for a book. The major problem with this model is that it locks in a very specific set of dates. What if the

---

[58] In Australia these are known respectively as the ABN (Australian Business No) and TFN (Tax File No). In the UK, the VAT No serves as a Business Identification No, and the UTR (Unique Taxpayer Reference) as a Taxpayer Identification No (although the NINO—National Insurance No—is also widely used).

number of review cycles is to be increased for some books? What about other key dates such as production of artwork, or production and review of the index? This model cannot handle these.

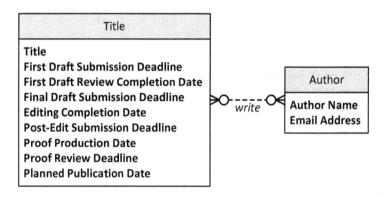

Figure 47: Publishing model (not recommended)

However, by generalizing all these date attributes, different sets of deadlines and completion dates can be arranged for different books if required. Note that unlike the other types of attribute generalization, this type always involves the creation of either (a) a **multi-valued composite attribute** as in Figure 48 or (b) a separate **dependent entity class**[59] as in Figure 49. Figure 50 is the UML class model equivalent of Figure 48.

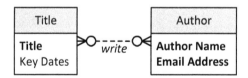

Figure 48: Flexible Publishing model with multi-valued composite attribute

---

[59] A **dependent entity class** is an entity class created to hold either (a) multiple values of a particular attribute of an entity instance, or (b) multiple sets of values of a particular set of attributes of an entity instance.

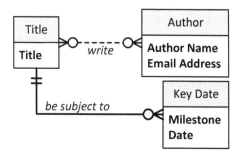

Figure 49: Flexible Publishing model with dependent entity class

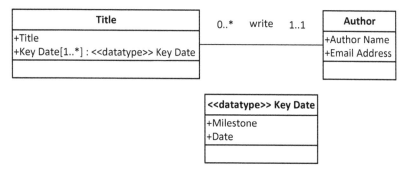

Figure 50: Flexible Publishing model in UML

6.7   Relationship generalization

You may recall the student administration system scenarios and requirements listed in Section 1.8 (summarized here):

- While every student has a biological mother and biological father, either or both of those parents may (a) be unknown, (b) be no longer involved in the student's education, (c) have a different family name from the student, or (d) reside at a different address from the student.

- There may be one, two, or more than two adults who have a parent/guardian role with respect to a student. If there are just two such adults, they may be of the same gender.

- It is essential to record for each student (a) two or more emergency contact phone numbers (including the sequence in which to call registered emergency contacts for a student) and (b) the e-mail address of each parent/guardian to support non-emergency contacts not delivered by mail.

- It is also essential to indicate whether each adult associated with the student is (a) wholly or partly liable for payment of school fees, (b) to receive academic reports, (c) to be invited to parent/teacher meetings, and/or (d) allowed to pick the student up from school.

One possible data model to support these requirements is shown in Figure 51. Notice the various roles a **Responsible Person** may have with respect to a **Student**. I have used the term Responsible Person rather than Adult since it is possible that an older sibling less than 18 years old may have some of these roles. You may wonder why I have marked the *be biological parent of* relationship as optional at the **Responsible Person** end: surely every **Student** has exactly two biological parents. Yes, this is true in the real world, but some Students may not know their biological father, and an orphan or adoptee may not know either biological parent. Thus, although there is a **real-world rule** that every Student has exactly two biological parents, there is no corresponding **data rule**.

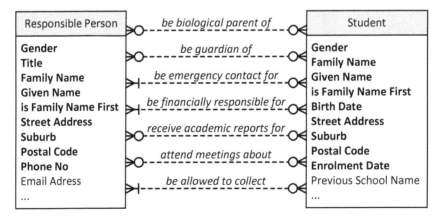

Figure 51: A better Student Administration data model

Surely we can generalize all those relationships, as in Figure 52? Yes, with the advantage that, if other roles that a Responsible Person may play with respect to a Student are required later, they can be accommodated without having to modify the model and the database. The only problem here is that we are no longer exposing the different roles in the way that the model in Figure 51 did.

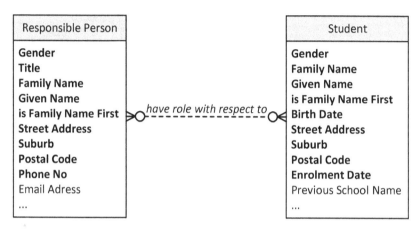

Figure 52: An even better Student Administration data model?

We have previously seen (in Section 5.9) that an n:n relationship can be replaced by an **intersection entity class**[60] and two 1:n relationships. If we do that here, we can now document the other attributes needed to support the requirements. Note that all the Boolean attributes (those with names starting "is") are mandatory: they must each have the value True or False. This assumes that, when a Student is enrolled, the Parent or Guardian enrolling them is required to provide this information for each nominated Responsible Person. If this is not the case, these attributes would have to be optional.

---

[60] An **intersection entity class** is an **n:n relationship** (see Section 5.4) represented using an **entity class**.

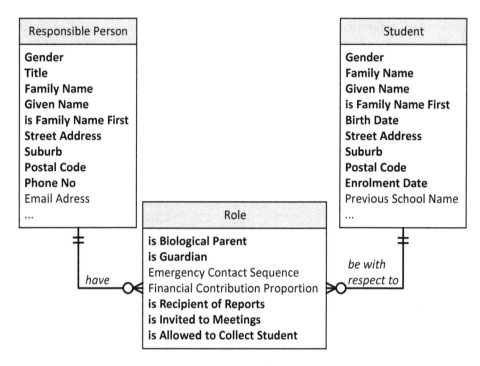

Figure 53: An even better Student Administration data model

By contrast, only those Responsible Persons on the Emergency Contact list would have their **Emergency Contact Sequence** recorded, and only Responsible Persons actually responsible for a financial contribution would have their **Financial Contribution Proportion** recorded.

6.8   Hierarchy generalization

Figure 54 is a model of the levels of US government, which might be used by an enterprise providing goods or services to government agencies.

What if the enterprise wishes to expand into Canada? There they have Provinces rather than States, and only Municipalities within Provinces. This presents us with a problem.

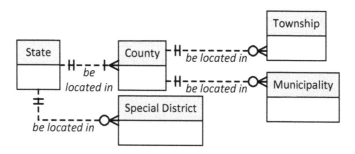

Figure 54: Specific levels of US government

One relatively simple solution would be to (a) redefine the **State** entity class to include also Canadian Provinces, (b) create a dummy **County** instance for each Canadian Province, and (c) add a **Country** entity class in which to record the federal governments of each country[61].

The more countries in which the enterprise operates, the more compromises need to be made, since each country organizes its levels and types of local jurisdiction differently. A more generic approach is illustrated in Figure 55.

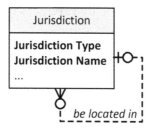

Figure 55: Generic levels of government

In this model, however, we have lost (a) the names of the various types of Jurisdiction, and (b) the rules governing which types of Jurisdiction can be located in which other types of Jurisdiction, all of which is useful information.

---

[61] This entity class should probably have been included even when the US was the only country within which sales were made.

The **Jurisdiction Type** attribute is used to specify whether a given Jurisdiction is a State, County, Township, Municipality, or Special District. The rules governing which types of Jurisdiction can be located in which other types of Jurisdiction will need to be either:

- explicitly documented as business rules, as discussed in Section 8.4.4.2, or

- recorded in a **Jurisdiction Type** entity class, with its own recursive relationship, which includes only allowable combinations of **Jurisdictions**, as in Figure 56[62].

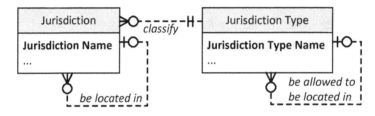

Figure 56: Generic levels of government with rules recorded in data

Another situation in which a generic hierarchy is better than a specific hierarchy is when modeling an enterprise's organization structure. An enterprise may currently be organized into Departments within Divisions but, given the possibility of reorganization, locking that structure into the data model would be unwise.

Modeling the organization structure as in Figure 56, but with entity classes **Organization Unit** and **Organization Unit Type** (with **Organization Unit Name** and **Organization Unit Type Name** attributes respectively), provides future-proofing.

---

[62] This is an example of **data-driven rules**, discussed in Section 8.8.

6.9   Summary

There are real-world concepts that share similarities but also differ by having different attributes and/or participating in different relationships. Subtypes are a useful means to document those similarities and differences.

Where attributes of role entity classes are similar, there may seem to be a case for generalizing them and transferring them to the associated **Party** entity class, but the disadvantages of doing so usually outweigh any advantages.

If attributes in different subtypes of the same supertype have the same meaning and the same name (or a name which business stakeholders understand and which accurately signifies both attributes), they can be generalized and transferred to the supertype.

Similar attributes in the same entity class may be generalized as either a multi-valued composite attribute or a separate dependent entity class.

Multiple relationships between the same entity classes may be generalized, resulting in a model that can accommodate further relationships that may be required in the future without needing to be changed.

Hierarchies can be represented either with specific entity classes at each level or with a single entity class and a recursive relationship.

Chapter 7.   Naming and defining model components

Whatever the purpose of a particular business information model[63], its function is to document the information of interest to the enterprise in a way that is understandable to business stakeholders. It is therefore essential that every entity class, attribute, and relationship in the model is named in a way that accurately reflects the artifact's meaning to the business.

If a business stakeholder has no idea what real-world concept an entity class is supposed to represent, that stakeholder will lose confidence in the validity of the model. However, in my experience, business stakeholders are often reluctant to confess to their lack of understanding. Even worse, a business stakeholder may think they know what real-world concept an entity class represents, when it actually means something else. This can arise if the name chosen has other meanings, as many words do.

7.1   Naming entity classes

7.1.1   Quality criteria for entity class names

A good entity class name meets the criteria on the following page:

---

[63] These purposes were listed in Section 1.6.1.

- It consists of one or more words, of which the last is a **countable noun** (a word that can occur between "each" and "may" in a grammatical sentence). Thus:

  - **Customer** is a countable noun, as "Each Customer may purchase up to ten of this Product" is a grammatical sentence, whereas
  - **Information** (a **non-countable noun**), **Motorized** (an **adjective**), and **Promote** (a **verb**) are not, as none of these words can occur between "each" and "may" in a grammatical sentence[64].

- The last word in the name may be preceded by other words such that the entire name is a meaningful business term, e.g., **Loyalty Program Customer**, **High-Value Customer**.

- That meaningful business term must:

  - signify *one* instance of the real-world concept that the entity class represents, e.g., **Customer** rather than **Customer Table** or **Customer File**
  - have a single consistent meaning across the business environment, i.e., the enterprise and its customer base (unlike **Line**: see Section 7.1.2)
  - not include any abbreviation unless (a) it has only one meaning across the business environment, and (b) it is familiar to all potential users of the model and any resulting application system.

An example of an abbreviation that has more than one meaning across the business environment is DOO which can mean either Day of Operation or Driver-Only Operation in the Australian railway industry.

---

[64] Note however that many adjectives and verbs can be used as nouns, e.g., notable, collective, run.

While some of these criteria facilitate understanding, other criteria are included to allow us to generate sentences from entity class and relationship names to facilitate verification of relationships, as described in Section 7.3.

7.1.2 Terms with multiple meanings

A good example of a term with multiple meanings across a business environment is **Line**, which railway operators in Australia use variously to refer to:

- a **corridor** containing one or more tracks, e.g., the Main West Line includes all tracks passing through Homebush and Strathfield (see Figure 57), and the Main North Line includes all tracks running North from Strathfield

- an individual **track** such as the Up Main (see Figure 57)

- one of the **color-coded lines** on the network map on display at stations and in trains. For example, in Figure 57:
  - the Up and Down North Main and North Suburban and the Up and Down Main and Suburban through Strathfield are part of the Red Line
  - the Up and Down Main through Homebush and the Up and Down Main and Suburban through Strathfield are part of the Yellow Line
  - the Up and Down Local and the Up and Down Suburban are part of the Blue Line.

Because of this, **Corridor** and **Track** are used as entity class names for the first two meanings in new data models, leaving **Line** for the third meaning. This is, of course, not ideal, but no term has emerged as an alternative for the third meaning.

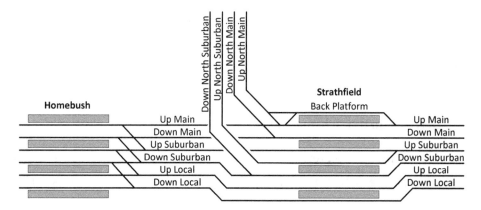

Figure 57: Part of a rail network

The commonly-understood term **Train** is similarly not recommended as an entity class name due to its various meanings:

- a coupled set of carriages or wagons, with or without one or more locomotives (known as a **Consist**)

- a timetabled service running between two or more stations on one or more days of the week (a **Trip**)

- a specific timetabled service running on a particular date (a **Dated Trip**).

There is a similar problem with the term **Flight** in the airline industry. QF1 is a service operated by the airline Qantas from Sydney to London Heathrow via Singapore. The term **Flight** may refer to:

- the entire daily Sydney-London service

- the daily Sydney–Singapore and Singapore–London services (also referred to as **Legs** or **Segments**)

- a Sydney–London, Sydney–Singapore or Singapore–London journey on a particular date.

Despite having multiple meanings, **Flight** is often used as an entity class name in the airline industry. If a term with multiple meanings appears as an entity class name, it is imperative that the definition of that entity class spells out clearly which meaning(s) are represented. Entity class definitions are discussed in Section 7.5.1.

7.1.3   What does each entity instance look like?

This is an important question. Consider a **Flight** entity:

- If it refers to a service that can land at intermediate airports and operates on one or more days, it needs relationships with two or more Airports, and a multi-valued attribute (or dependent entity class) to record the Days of Operation.

- If it refers to a Leg or Segment (i.e., no landings at intermediate airports) that operates on one or more days, it needs relationships with just two Airports, and a multi-valued attribute (or dependent entity class) to record the Days of Operation. We should also name the entity class **Leg** or **Segment**.

- If it refers to a service on a particular date, it needs relationships with two or more (or just two) Airports, and a Date attribute. We should also name the entity class **Dated Flight**, **Dated Leg**, or **Dated Segment** as appropriate.

We need to check with business stakeholders which meaning applies before we proceed, then document that in the definition of the entity class[65].

Another term that can have subtly different meanings is **Part**, found in Stock Control (Inventory) system data models. Some enterprises use or supply

---

[65] See Section 7.5.1.

Rotables and Repairables[66], which are parts that can be refurbished (or repaired) and redeployed. Examples in the airline industry include wheels, brakes, and items of electronic equipment. These must be individually tracked, so their Serial Numbers must be recorded, and there must be a record for each individual Part. By contrast, Consumables (Expendables) do not need Serial numbers and only need a single record for each set of similar Parts, with a count of how many of that Part are in store, and a unique description. The description of a Non-Consumable will be the same for each record of a Part of the same type, so should be moved to a separate **Non-Consumable Part Type** entity.

7.1.4   Terms with specialized meanings

Some terms have specialized meanings in particular industries or government service sectors. The term **Parcel** has a specific meaning to Australia Post[67], the same meaning as understood by the general public, but to Australian Land Registries and to the conveyancing industry, it refers to a defined piece of real estate. This term can be used as an entity class name in either context, since within each context it has a consistent meaning across the business environment.

7.1.5   General and specific names

It is important not to select names for entity classes that are too specific. One airline has used an entity class named **Port** (the industry-standard term) to represent not only airports but other locations, including city terminals and holiday islands without airports. Fortunately, there was general understanding

---

[66] The distinction between Rotables and Repairables is concerned with the lifetime of the Part and has little or no impact on what data is required.

[67] The Australian postal service.

within the airline that all these were included. Meanwhile, a European airline which realized that fast trains were a more effective means of travel than aircraft between reasonably-close cities started including train services in the **Flight** entity class, even giving them **Flight Nos**!

An alternative approach is to identify the future scope of an entity class and agree on a term that covers all current and potential instances. I'm not sure that **Transport Location** and **Transport Service** would have been more acceptable than **Port** and **Flight**, but it would be worth trying.

We've already seen a very common generalized name: **Party** covering Persons and Organizations. All enterprises for which I've developed data models have seen the benefit of including this general concept and have accepted **Party** as the name, albeit sometimes with some initial reluctance.

7.1.6   Subtype names

A subtype is an entity class in its own right, so each subtype must have a name that meets the criteria for an entity class name listed in Section 7.1.1. In particular, a subtype name should *not* just be an adjective. I have encountered models in which, for example, the **Road Vehicle** supertype has **Powered** and **Non-Powered** as subtypes. In Section 7.3, we shall see that a method for verifying relationships is to construct sentences from the names of the relationship and the related entity classes. This method relies on *all* entity class names meeting the listed criteria.

7.2   Naming attributes

In a business information model, each attribute should be named according to the assigned attribute class, as follows:

- **identifier attribute**: **No**, **Code**, or **Name** preceded by either the entity class name (e.g., **Customer No**, **Product Code**) or some synonym thereof (e.g., **Registered Business Name**)

- **Boolean attribute**: **is** followed by the relevant condition, e.g., **is Family Name First**

- **set selection attribute**: a name that (a) would be used by the business to refer to a member of the relevant set, and (b) meets the criteria for an entity class name (see Section 7.1.1), e.g., **Gender**, **Travel Class**, **Payment Method**

- **descriptor attribute**: **Description**, **Comment**, or some other *singular* noun (*not* **Remarks** or **Comments**, as these might be confused with multi-valued attributes)

- single point-in-time attributes:
    - **datetime**: **Date and Time** preceded by one or more qualifying terms, e.g., **Transaction Date and Time**
    - **date**: **Date** preceded by one or more qualifying terms, e.g., **Birth Date** of a **Customer** (or followed by **of** and the name of some event, e.g., **Date of Birth**)
    - **year number**: **Year** preceded by one or more qualifying terms, e.g., **Model Year** of a **Road Vehicle**

- recurrent point-in-time attributes:
    - **day of week**: **Day** preceded by one or more qualifying terms, e.g., **Rostered Absence Day**
    - **time of day**: **Time** preceded by one or more qualifying terms, e.g., **Timetabled Arrival Time**
    - **time of week**: **Time** preceded by one or more qualifying terms, e.g., **Start Time** of a **Program** on a TV station
    - **day of week of month**: **Day** preceded by one or more qualifying terms, e.g., **Timesheet Submission Day**
    - **time of week of month**: **Time** preceded by one or more qualifying terms, e.g., **Meeting Start Time**
    - **day of month**: **Date** or **Day** preceded by one or more qualifying terms, e.g., **Mortgage Repayment Date**

- o **day of year**: **Date** or **Day** preceded by one or more qualifying terms, e.g., **Birthday** of a **Customer**[68].

- **monetary amount**: **Amount**, **Price**, **Balance**, **Extension**, etc. as appropriate, preceded by one or more qualifying terms, e.g., **Transaction Amount**, **Unit Price**, **Current Balance**

- **dimensioned quantifier** other than monetary amount: either:

  - o **Distance**, **Length**, **Width**, **Height**, **Mass**, **Weight**, **Duration**, **Speed**, **Temperature**, **Voltage**, **Frequency**, etc. as appropriate, preceded by one or more qualifying terms if required, e.g.,
    - **Sighting Distance** of a **Railway Signal**
    - **Overall Length**, **Overall Width**, **Overall Height**, **Gross Vehicle Mass**, and **Maximum Laden Weight** of a **Vehicle**
    - **Duration** of a **Monthly Meeting**
    - **Normal Cruising Speed** of an **Aircraft Type**
    - **Maximum Operating Temperature** of an **Equipment Item**
    - **Voltage** and **Frequency** of a **Power Supply**, or

  - o a commonly-used and understood term for the quantity, e.g.,
    - **Mileage Allowance** of a **Vehicle Rental Agreement**
    - **Quantity Ordered**, **Quantity Received** of an **Order Item**
    - **Reorder Point** of a **Stock Item**
    - **Minimum Headway** of a **Track Section** in an urban transit system
    - **Maximum Service Interval** of a **Peak Service** in an urban transit system

- **count** (cardinal number): either:

  - o **Number of** followed by name of item being counted, e.g., **Number of Axles**, or
  - o **Quantity** preceded by one or more qualifying terms, e.g., **Order Quantity**

---

[68] Compare this with **Birth Date**.

- **sequence number** (ordinal number): **Sequence No**, **Sequence**, or **No**, preceded by one or more qualifying terms, e.g., **Task Sequence No**, **Emergency Contact Sequence**, **Period No** (in a school timetabling system)

- **ratio/rate/factor**: **Ratio**, **Rate**, **Factor**, **Concentration**, etc. as appropriate, preceded by one or more qualifying terms, e.g., **Price Earnings Ratio** (of a **Stock**), **Reproduction Rate** (of a **Disease**), **Expansion Factor** (of a **Fluid**), **Oxygen Concentration** (of a **Water Sample**)

- **image**: **Image**, **Photograph**, **Map**, **Chart**, or **Diagram**, preceded by one or more qualifying terms, e.g., **Scanned Passport Image**, **Employee Photograph**

- **sound** or **video recording**: **Recording**, preceded by one or more qualifying terms, e.g., **Customer Interaction Recording**

- **composite attribute**[69]: a name that (a) would be used by the business to refer to a member of the relevant attribute, and (b) meets the criteria for an entity class name (see Section 7.1.1), e.g., **Address**, **Person Name**

- **multi-valued attribute**[70]: the *plural* form of the name you would give the corresponding single-valued attribute, e.g., **Days of Operation**, **Meals**.

In selecting the qualifying terms for an attribute name, it's a good idea to use generalized rather than country-specific terms. For example, a US data modeler might be tempted to use **Zip Code** as an attribute name, which is fine if the application system being modeled is only ever going to operate in the US. Other countries have different terms for the corresponding codes, e.g., **Postcode** in Australia. A more generalized name is **Postal Code**. Similarly, the numbers used to identify taxpayers and businesses are given different names in different countries. In Section 6.6.1, I used the names **Taxpayer Identification No** and **Business Identification No** rather than the names used in Australia (**Tax File No** and **Australian Business No**).

---

[69] See Section 4.4.

[70] See Section 4.5.

Following this attribute naming standard will help you to avoid ambiguous attribute names like:

- **Discount** in a **Transaction** entity class, which could mean either the Discount Amount (e.g., $10) or the Discount Rate (e.g., 10%)

- **Date** in an **Invoice** entity class, which could mean either the Date the Invoice was raised or the Date by which payment is required.

7.3   Naming relationships

There are three approaches to relationship naming, each based on a particular form of verb phrase:

- an **infinitive verb phrase** is one that can immediately follow 'must' or 'may' in a grammatical sentence, e.g., *raise, include, be responsible for* (as in "each Customer may *raise* more than one Order", "each Order must *include* at least one Order Item", and "a Responsible Person may *be responsible for* more than one Student")

- a **third-person singular present indicative verb phrase** is one that can legitimately occur between two entity class names each preceded by 'a' or 'an' in a grammatical sentence, e.g., *raises, includes, is responsible for* (as in "a Customer *raises* an Order", "an Order *includes* an Order Item", and "a Responsible Person *is responsible for* a Student")

- a third school of thought limits the verb phrases used to name relationships to those that start with 'be' or 'is' and removes the 'be' or 'is', e.g., *responsible for* (rather than *be responsible for* or *is responsible for*).

The obvious problem with the third approach is that it forces the modeler either to:

- use only the passive form of the appropriate verb phrase (e.g., *raised by, included in*), or

- concoct unwieldy names for relationships that express actions (such as *raise*) or relationships that can be expressed with a simple verb (such as *include*). For example, the relationship between **Customer** and **Order** could be named *initiator of*, and the relationship between **Order** and **Order Item** could be named *container of*, neither of which reflects how the business might refer to these relationships.

My preference is for the first approach, i.e., infinitive verb phrases. This enables us to construct sentences from the names of the relationship and associated entity classes, which we can then use to verify the meaning, cardinalities, and optionalities of each relationship. For example, the relationships in Figure 58 can be verbalized as:

- Each **Country** may *have granted citizenship to* one or more **Persons**.
  Each **Person** may *be a citizen of* one or more **Countries**.

- Each **Country** must *be the location of* at least one **City/Town**.
  Each **City/Town** must *be located in* exactly one **Country**.

- Each **City/Town** may *be the birthplace of* one or more **Persons**.
  Each **Person** must *be born in* exactly one **City/Town**.

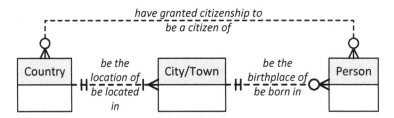

Figure 58: Birth and Citizenship

The second approach can be used in a similar way to construct sentences but, in this case, the use of *is* rather than *be* results in the following verbalizations:

- Each **Country** *has granted citizenship to* zero, one, or more **Persons**.
  Each **Person** *is a citizen of* zero, one, or more **Countries**.

- Each **Country** *is the location of* at least one **City/Town**.
  Each **City/Town** *is located in* exactly one **Country**.

- Each **City/Town** *is the birthplace of* zero, one, or more **Persons**.
  Each **Person** *is born in* exactly one **City/Town**.

I have a problem with "zero, one, or more". If we deconstruct the first relationship sentence, we get:

Each **Country** *has granted citizenship to* zero **Persons**, one **Person**, or more than one **Person**.

Business stakeholders (unlike mathematicians and some data modelers) tend not to say "each Country has granted citizenship to zero Persons". Indeed, Graeme Simsion wrote in (Simsion & Witt, 2004), "'Zero or more' is an expression only a programmer could love, and our aim is to communicate with business specialists in a natural way without sacrificing precision."

Your data modeling tool may have the capability to automatically generate relationship sentences from entity class and relationship names. If so, it probably dictates which naming approach to use so that the generated sentences are grammatical. Above all, you need to name relationships *consistently*. I often see models with a mix of relationship naming conventions, which makes automatic sentence generation impossible and manual generation trickier.

7.3.1   Relationship names in diagrams

In Figure 58, each relationship has been given a name in *both* directions, whereas, in other diagrams, there is only one name for each relationship.

When adding a relationship to a model, you should create a suitable name in each direction. This enables most data modeling tools to use these names in sentences describing rules, which are useful when business stakeholders are reviewing models.

However, to avoid clutter in diagrams, it is a good idea to display only one name for each relationship (generally the shorter of the two). Ideally, your data modeling tool will allow you to:

- record both names of each relationship in appropriate metadata fields, and
- decide which of the two names is to appear in diagrams.

Whether one or both names are displayed, there is a convention dictating which side of the relationship line a name appears. This is to enable anyone viewing the diagram to correctly infer the sentence(s) describing the relationship. If you view the two entity class names and the relationship name(s) as being located on an ellipse (as illustrated in Figure 59):

- start with one entity class name
- if there is no relationship name that appears in a clockwise direction around the ellipse, switch to the other entity class name
- construct the sentence by using the selected entity class name, the relationship name that appears in a clockwise direction around the ellipse, and the other entity class name.

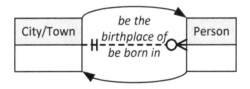

Figure 59: Reading relationship names

7.4 Using a taxonomic glossary to manage names

Most data modeling projects dive in at the deep end and are soon simultaneously grappling with six questions:

1. What real-world concepts are we talking about?

2. How do they differ?

3. In what ways are different real-world concepts similar?

4. How should we name each real-world concept?

5. What properties of these real-world concepts are of interest?

6. What associations between these real-world concepts are of interest?

The exercise can be made a lot easier by separating the first four questions from the other two, and developing a taxonomic glossary to organize business terminology.

This sounds like extra effort, and it is. If such a glossary were developed for only one project, it might not be cost-effective. However, more and more enterprises are starting to appreciate the benefits of developing glossaries to manage *all* terminology use, not only in technology (application systems, webpages, etc.) but in written communication such as procedure manuals. If all user interfaces use consistent terminology, customers and internal users are more likely to supply consistent data and more likely to understand data retrieved. If all data models use consistent terminology, integration of data resources is easier and less error-prone.

Once a glossary has been developed, entity class names should be selected from that glossary. If the obvious name for an entity class is absent from the glossary, it should be added.

7.4.1   Why a taxonomic glossary?

Many business glossaries are alphabetically organized, and therefore of little use to those who do not know the correct term to use. If someone is searching for the correct term, they either have to search the entire glossary or make a series of guesses, unless non-approved terms are also listed with cross-references to the correct term. For example, if we are looking for the correct term for a party's ownership of real estate in a land registry, we might suspect it could be **Ownership**, but it could be **Proprietorship**, so we look for each in turn. If the correct term is **Tenancy**, we won't find it (short of searching over three quarters of the glossary) unless the other terms are included with the notation "see **Tenancy**".

7.4.2   What does a taxonomic glossary look like?

A taxonomic glossary organizes terms as a taxonomy, with a small set of top-level classes, each with a hierarchy of more specific classes. Figure 60 is a screenshot from the home page of a taxonomic glossary I developed as a set of hyperlinked Microsoft Excel workbooks for an Australian land registry. It displays 10 top-level classes and the subclasses of each. Definitions of these top-level classes appear in Section 7.5.1.2.

Definitions and additional levels in the hierarchy are displayed when a class name is clicked, as in Figure 61. At these levels, the + and − icons are used to show or hide lower levels.

Similar glossaries were subsequently adopted by other government agencies, each including different sets of terms under each of the top-level terms (reflecting its particular interests and scope of operations).

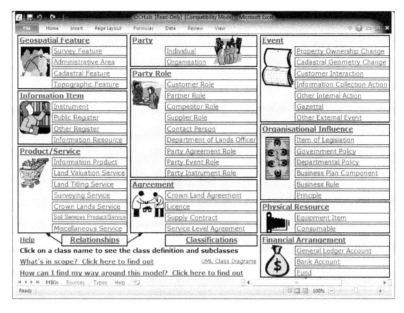

Figure 60: The top two levels of a taxonomic glossary

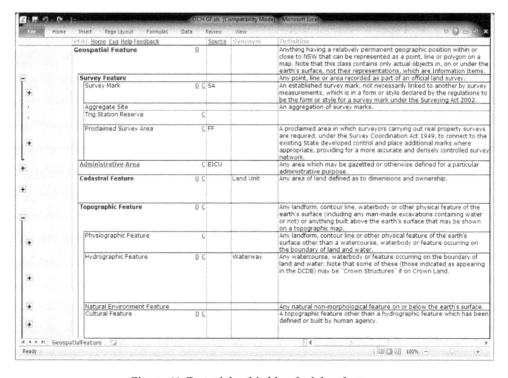

Figure 61: Part of the third level of the glossary

I subsequently produced a simpler taxonomic glossary in Microsoft Word for an urban rail transport operator, a fragment of which is depicted in Figure 62.

Entity					Definition	Use Case
Nodal Geography Concept					a concept relevant to the network of tracks on which trains may run	
	Node				(aka Location) a defined location on the rail network referenced in public or working timetables	[SUC4.3]
		Macro Node			a Node at the macro level of the Nodal Geography	
			Station		a location on the rail network where passengers can board or alight from trains and which appears on customer-facing maps and public timetables	[SUC7.6]
			Junction		a location at which trains can be routed to alternative final or intermediate destinations	
			Yard		a location where rolling stock can be stored between trips, or where freight (including coal) trains can be loaded, unloaded and/or marshalled	[SUC5]
				Stabling Location	(aka Storage Location) a location where passenger rolling stock can be stored and/or maintained between trips	[SUC5]
				Stabling Yard	(aka Car Sidings, Out Depot) a location where passenger rolling stock can be stored between trips	[SUC5]
				Maintenance Centre	a designated location where maintenance work is carried out on rolling stock	[SUC5]
			Freight Yard		a location where freight trains can be loaded, unloaded and/or marshalled	
			Colliery		a location where coal trains can be loaded	
			Power Station		a location where coal trains can be unloaded for power generation	
			Coal Terminal		a location where coal trains can be unloaded for export	
		Boundary Point			a location at which control passes from one Rail Infrastructure Manager to another	

Figure 62: Fragment of a rail transport taxonomic glossary

Note (a) the inclusion of various synonyms (alternative terms with the same meaning) and (b) cross-references to **Use Cases**, which formed part of the **requirements specification**[71] for this project.

Taxonomic glossaries are common as part of, or support for, industry standard data models, such as can be found in the airline and financial services industries among others.

Each term in the glossary should be given a definition that meets the same criteria as for an entity class definition (see Section 7.5.1). Synonyms should be listed, as in Figure 61 or Figure 62.

---

[71] See Section 10.3.1.

7.5   Entity class and attribute definitions

An entity class's name alone may not be sufficient to make clear what real-world objects are covered by that entity class.

Similarly, an attribute's name may not be sufficient for a developer or user to understand what values that attribute may hold and what those values mean.

Therefore both entity classes and attributes should be given definitions. I'm not aware of any data modeling tool that displays these definitions in a data model diagram—if it did, the diagram would be so cluttered as to be useless as a means of communication. Instead, all tools produce data model reports, in which entity classes, attributes, and relationships can be listed along with relevant **metadata**[72] such as definitions.

7.5.1   Entity class definitions

Each entity class (including subtypes) must have a definition that clearly and unambiguously defines which objects are and are not included in the scope of the entity class.

If you have developed a glossary as described in Section 7.4 and selected all entity class names from that glossary, you will have a ready-made definition which will meet the criteria set out in this section. If you have decided not to develop a glossary, you will have to define each entity class now using those criteria.

---

[72] **Metadata** is data about data.

The definition of an entity class may be:

- **intensional**, in which the objects included in the scope of the entity class are defined as members of a more general class with one or more distinguishing characteristics, e.g., **Minor**: a Person whose age is less than the age of majority, or

- **extensional**, in which the objects covered by the business term are listed, e.g., **Minor**: a Boy or a Girl.

Each definition should initially be sourced from the following (in sequence):

1. any existing business glossary

2. any procedural documentation produced by the enterprise

3. any relevant legislation

4. a specialized dictionary (if any) for the industry in which the enterprise operates

5. a general dictionary of the natural language in use within the enterprise, e.g., English[73].

Once a working definition has been found, it should be reviewed with business stakeholders.

7.5.1.1   Quality criteria for entity class definitions

Each entity class definition should meet the following criteria:

- Each definition must be unambiguous.

---

[73] If a general dictionary is used to source a definition for an entity class name that has multiple meanings, take care to pick the definition for the appropriate meaning. A junior modeler tasked with producing entity class definitions rightly decided that the "social gathering" meaning was inappropriate in a definition of Party but then used the definition "an organization of people with particular political beliefs that competes in elections to try to win positions in local or national government" much to the amusement of business stakeholders.

- No definition should be misleading, in the sense that any reader might infer either:
  - inclusion of inappropriate instances in the set represented by the entity class (if the definition is too general), or
  - inappropriate exclusion of some instances from that set (if the definition is too specific).

- Each definition must use natural language syntax, so that "A <term> is a <definition>" forms a grammatical sentence. For example, "a Party who lends money under the terms of a Mortgage" is appropriate as a definition of **Mortgagee** since "A Mortgagee is a Party who lends money under the terms of a Mortgage" is a grammatical sentence.

- The definition should include at least one 'a', 'an', or 'any' (rather than 'the'). For example, "*the* Party who lends money under the terms of *a* Mortgage" is an acceptable alternative definition of **Mortgagee**, but "*the* Party who lends money under the terms of *the* Mortgage" is not.

- The terms (noun phrases) used in the definition should be either:
  - other entity class names (in which case they should be marked in some way, at the very least rendered with initial capitals (as with Party and Mortgage in the example above), or
  - terms which have a single generally-understood meaning among the audience(s) for the model.

- No entity class should be defined in terms of any data item or information resource representing that entity class. For example, the entity class **Customer** should not be defined as "a Party recorded in the Customer Database" but instead be defined in terms of the events and/or relationships that characterize a customer in the real world, e.g., "a Party who has purchased, or is purchasing, goods or services from the enterprise."

- If appropriate, examples of instances of the entity class may be listed at the end of the definition after the words "such as" or "for example". For example, the definition of **Regulatory Agency** in an airline data model might be "a Public Authority or Government Agency responsible for exercising authority over some area of the enterprise's activity in a regulatory or supervisory capacity to enforce safety and standards, protect consumers, etc., for example the Federal Aviation Administration."

An entity class's name may be open to misinterpretation in that there may be concepts or instances that one could reasonably infer were represented by the entity class but which should instead be included in a different entity class. If so, these should be documented either (a) in a separate free text metadata field from the definition (if available), or (b) as an addition to the definition (if no other field is available), each with the appropriate other entity class name. This is particularly important where it may not be clear whether the entity class represents individual objects or classes of objects. For example, entity classes named **Aircraft** are commonly used to represent either:

- individual aircraft, each with a separate tail number (registration number), as in "ten aircraft landed at Vancouver airport between 0900 and 1000 today", or

- aircraft models (e.g., 'Airbus 380'), as in "which aircraft does this airline operate?"

The entity class **Aircraft** should therefore have, in addition to its definition, a statement that it does not include aircraft models, which are represented instead by the entity class **Aircraft Model**.

7.5.1.2 Some examples

These are the definitions of the top-level terms in Figure 60:

- **Party**: a person or organization (not necessarily legally constituted) that may play one or more Party Roles

- **Party Role**: a role played by a Party with respect to the enterprise (e.g., Customer, Employee, Supplier, Service Provider, Partner, Regulator) or some Arrangement or Event (e.g., Vendor, Purchaser, Applicant)

- **Geospatial Feature**: any place where the enterprise or its customers or suppliers operates, any physical address to or from which goods or communications may be sent, or any geopolitical or organizational division of the earth's surface (e.g., Country, State, Region, City, Postal Zone, Building, Room, Port, Terminal, Gate, Physical Address)

- **Product/Service**: any product or service that the enterprise provides to Customers

- **Physical Resource**: any equipment item, building, furniture, or consumable used by the enterprise in its operations

- **Arrangement**: any agreement, contract, or other ongoing arrangement, such as a Lease, Insurance Policy, Program, or Project, in which the enterprise is involved or has an interest

- **Event**: anything that happens that affects the enterprise, such as a Customer or Supplier activity, a process performed by a Staff Member, or a Financial Transaction

- **Organizational Influence**: anything which influences the actions of the enterprise, its Staff Members and/or its Customers, or how those actions are performed, such as Items of Legislation, Regulations, Policies, Business Plans, Performance Indicators, Standard Amounts and Rates, Business Rules, and external issues (political, industrial, social, economic, demographic, or environmental) that influence the operation or behavior of the enterprise

- **Information Resource**: any set or item of information maintained or used by the enterprise, such as a Record, File, Database, Inter-System Message, or Data Item therein.

7.5.2   Attribute definitions

If the business information model is to be effectively reviewed, reviewers need to be sure of the meaning and purpose of each attribute. In some cases, the attribute name may be sufficient to convey this, but for many attributes the name alone may not be sufficient. For that reason, I prefer to provide *every* attribute with a definition that makes clear its meaning and purpose.

Unfortunately, this adds to the effort required to develop the model, so I've often observed others take shortcuts, even when the enterprise standard is that every attribute has a definition[74]. One data modeling tool gives each attribute an automatic definition based on the entity class and attribute names, e.g., (for the **Family Name** attribute of the **Person** entity class) "Family Name is of Person", which gives no one any additional information.

Meaningful attribute definitions are not only required for effective review of the model. Columns in the logical data model inherit definitions from their source attributes (as described in Section 11.2). Those column definitions enable developers to understand the meaning of each column and thus to develop appropriate code to use or update column values. And, as described above, those column definitions (if meaningful) can be a useful resource for application system users.

Figure 63 includes some examples of attribute definitions that I included in a recent data model for an Australian urban transport operator:

---

[74] At one site I discovered that every attribute had been given the definition "X". Unfortunately at least one application system displayed the attribute definition if the user hovered the mouse pointer over the corresponding on-screen field!

Entity Class	Multiple Unit Type
Definition	a class of permanently-coupled self-propelled passenger-carrying rolling stock with a common specification
Attribute	Definition
Unit Type Code	the code preceding the Unit No displayed at each end of a unit of this type
Number of Cars	the number of cars in a unit of this type
Seated Capacity	the number of seats in a unit of this type
Outline Gauge	the width code defined in the Train Operating Manual for units of this type: one of 'N' (Narrow), 'M' (Medium), 'E' (Extended Medium), 'W' (Wide)
Propulsion	the method of propulsion of units of this type: one of 'Diesel', 'Electric'
Transmission Type	if **Propulsion** is 'Diesel', the method of transmitting power from the power unit to wheelsets: one of 'Hydraulic', 'Mechanical', 'Electric'
Axle Load	the maximum axle load of a unit of this type, in kg
Unit Length	the length of a unit of this type, in kg
Unit Weight	the weight of a unit of this type, in kg
Speed Band	the code defined in the Train Operating Manual for this unit type, based on acceleration and braking characteristics and used to determine feasible and safe operating speeds on each part of the rail network

Figure 63: Attribute definitions

7.6   Summary

Entity class names may be open to misinterpretation. It is therefore important that each entity class be given a definition that clearly and unambiguously defines which objects are and are not included in the scope of the entity class. Subtypes are entity classes, so must also be defined.

Attribute names may also be open to misinterpretation. Adherence to an attribute naming standard can help to avoid ambiguous attribute names.

Using infinitive verb phrases to name relationships enables construction of sentences from entity class and relationship names to verify the correctness of each relationship and its cardinalities and optionalities.

Each entity class definition must use natural language syntax to clearly and unambiguously define which objects are and are not included in the scope of that entity class.

Each attribute definition must make clear the meaning and purpose of that attribute.

Chapter 8.   Business rules

As with so many concepts in IT, there are numerous definitions of the term **business rule** (some conflicting). The one that makes the most sense to me—since it is one of the few that covers *all* business rules—is Barbara von Halle's 2001 definition: *"a condition that govern[s] … business event[s] so that [they] occur in such a way that is acceptable to the business."*

There are various ways of categorizing business rules, one of which makes the following distinction:

- **operative rules**[75] define what must or must not happen in particular circumstances, e.g., "Each **Flight Booking Request** must specify exactly one **Departure Date**."
  Operative rules can be contravened—the person requesting the booking can omit that information—but, in a well-designed system, such contraventions result in the process being paused until the rule is complied with.

- **definitional rules**[76] define constructs created by the enterprise, the industry within which it operates, or the scientific or business community, e.g., "**Close of business** is by definition 5pm", "**pH** is by definition between 0 and 14 inclusive".
  By their nature, definitional rules cannot be contravened.

---

[75] These are also known as **normative** or **prescriptive** rules.
[76] These are also known as **descriptive** or **structural** rules.

In (Witt, 2012) I further categorized operative rules as:

- **data rules**, which constrain the data included in a transaction, form, message, or persistent data set such as a database, e.g., "The **Number of Passengers** specified in each **Flight Booking Request** must be at least 1."

- **activity rules**, which constrain the operation of business processes or other activities, e.g., "Online Check-in for a Flight may occur only during the 24 hours before the Departure Time of that Flight."

- **party rules**, which restrict the parties who can perform a process or activity or play a role, e.g., "A Person may be rostered on a Flight Crew only if that Person holds an Airline Transport Pilot License that is current and a Type Endorsement that is current for each Aircraft Type to be flown by that Flight Crew."

The only rules that concern us as data modelers are data rules and **decision rules** (a particular subclass of activity rules, discussed in Section 8.7). Sections 8.1 to 8.6 discuss data rules in detail, as they exhibit considerable variety. For example:

- many attributes are **mandatory**: they must be present for all instances of the entity class they describe, e.g., every Customer must have a Name

- some attributes can only have numeric values, and of these:
  - some can only have positive values, e.g., **Order Quantity**
  - some may only have non-negative values, e.g., **Number of Children** in a **Flight Booking Request** may be zero
  - some may be limited to a specific range of values, e.g., **Number of Passengers** in a **Flight Booking Request** is limited to the range 1 to 9 inclusive[77]

---

[77] Arguably the first truly computerized airline reservation system was Sabre, released in 1964 when storage was significantly more expensive than today. A decision taken in the design of

  o   some can only have **integer** (whole number) values, e.g., **Number of Seats** in an **Automobile**

- any attribute including a date can only include valid date values

- any attribute including a time can only include valid time values

- a Boolean attribute can only have the values True, False, and (in some cases) Unknown

- a set selection attribute (see Section 4.7.3) can only have values from the relevant list, e.g., **Payment Type** in some situations can only be Credit Card, Debit Card, or Direct Debit

- relationships are governed by **cardinality** and **optionality** but also other rules (see Section 8.4).

8.1   When should data rules be documented?

All rules governing each attribute and relationship in the logical data model must be documented before that model can be considered to be complete. There are two ways this can be done:

- Document all data rules in the business information model. This has the advantage that they can be reviewed by business stakeholders in conjunction with the business information model, so an additional business review cycle is not required at the completion of logical data modeling. The disadvantage of this approach is that it takes longer to produce the business information model. For this reason, if multiple reviews of the business information model have been planned, it makes sense to (a) produce a model without data rules for the first of those reviews, and (b) include the data rules in a subsequent review.

---

that system, to use only one digit for the number of passengers, appears to have continued to influence successor systems.

- Defer data rule documentation to the logical data modeling phase. This means that an additional business review is required during that phase, but has the advantage that the business information model can be delivered sooner as time does not have to be spent identifying, analyzing, and documenting data rules.

Irrespective of when they are documented, all data rules need to be reviewed by business stakeholders, so they must be documented in a business-friendly manner to allow for that review.

If you decide to document data rules in the logical data model but encounter some during business information modeling, record them in a separate document rather than the model. This document should clarify that it doesn't list all rules, to avoid giving reviewers the impression that there are no other rules.

Section 8.6 describes how to document data rules.

8.2 Rule statements

In the remainder of this chapter, various **rule statements** are used to illustrate different types of rule. A rule statement is a sentence in an appropriate natural language (English in this case) and has become the preferred means of communicating business rules. The rule statements in this book are based on the rule statement language published in (Witt, 2012), which was based on the meta-rules for such a language that were published in the version of (Object Management Group, 2019) current at that time.

To distinguish rule statements from the general discussion in the rest of this chapter, each is a complete sentence in a box. For example:

Each **Order** must specify exactly one **Payment Method**.

If a rule statement includes a relationship name, that name appears in italics. Verb phrases used to associate attributes with entity classes (e.g., 'has', 'specify') are rendered in plain text.

8.3   Attribute rules

This section covers all rules governing attributes except uniqueness rules (covered in Section 8.5).

8.3.1   Attribute cardinality rules

This section covers all rules governing the presence, absence, or allowed numbers of attributes.

8.3.1.1   Mandatory attribute rules

Some attributes of real-world concepts are **mandatory**, in that every instance of that concept has that attribute. For example, each person, living or deceased, has a date of birth. By contrast, while each deceased person has a date of death, living persons do not yet have one.

It is important to realize the distinction between **real-world rules** and **data rules**. In the real world, every person has a birth date. However, in the data world, the enterprise may record data about a person but not include that person's birth date. This could be because it is not essential to the enterprise's dealings with that person (for example, Facebook allows a user to supply their birth date, but that is optional).

To summarize, each attribute has one of three possible cardinalities:

- attributes that are mandatory in data, e.g.

> Each **Employee** has a **Family Name**, which must be recorded against that **Employee**.

- attributes that are mandatory in the real world but optional in data, e.g.

> Each **Employee** has a **Birth Date**, which may be omitted from the record of that **Employee**.

- attributes that are optional in the real world, e.g.

> Each **Employee** may or may not have a **Middle Initial**.

How do you distinguish these three situations in a data model? Data modeling tools only make the distinction between mandatory and optional. I recommend that in your data modeling tool you:

- mark only those attributes that are mandatory *in data* as mandatory

- indicate whether the attribute is mandatory or optional in the real world in either the definition field or some other free text metadata field available in the tool.

The second step may seem like additional effort for no benefit. However, if you don't include that information, automatic generation of statements to describe the model (see Section 10.5.2) would lead to statements like "Each **Employee** may or may not have a **Birth Date**" which reviewers are likely to reject.

Even where an enterprise needs to know a person's birth date, there may be people who do not remember their birth dates. I once designed a public health database that was tracking health outcomes categorized by various demographics, including age. However, many subjects were elderly and could not remember the year they were born (even if they could remember the month and day of month), or could remember the year but weren't sure of the month or day. The implications of this are discussed in Section 8.3.2.7.

8.3.1.2 Conditional mandatory attribute rules

Some attributes can be mandatory only under certain conditions. For example, while a Flight Booking Request for a Return Journey must specify a Return Date, the **Return Date** attribute is not simply mandatory, as it is not required for a One-Way Journey. The attribute is only mandatory for a Return Journey:

> Each **Flight Booking Request** for a **Return Journey** must specify exactly one **Return Date**.

Conditional mandatory data rules are particularly important if you model a supertype without its subtypes, as illustrated in Figure 40 in Section 6.1. In that model, various attributes are marked as optional but are mandatory for particular subtypes, e.g.

> Each **Road Vehicle** in which **Vehicle Type** is Bus must specify exactly one **Number of Standing Passengers**.

> Each **Road Vehicle** in which **Vehicle Type** is other than Trailer must specify exactly one **Propulsion Type**.

> Each **Road Vehicle** in which **Vehicle Type** is Automobile, Utility Vehicle, or Bus must specify exactly one **Number of Seats**.

We previously encountered a conditionally mandatory attribute in Section 5.9:

> An **Annual Union Dues Amount** must be specified for each **Employee** that belongs to a **Union**.

8.3.1.3   Prohibited attribute rules

Not only is a Return Date not required for a One-Way Journey, it makes no sense to include one. If a customer has included one, an error message should be displayed, prompting the customer to either delete the Return Date or change the Journey Type to Return Journey.

> A **Flight Booking Request** for a **One-Way Journey** must not specify a **Return Date**.

Again, prohibited data rules are important if you model a supertype without its subtypes, e.g.

> A **Road Vehicle** in which **Vehicle Type** is Trailer must not specify a **Propulsion Type**.

And, referring again to Section 5.9,

> An **Annual Union Dues Amount** must not be specified for any **Employee** that does not *belong to* a **Union**.

As with each of these examples, prohibited attribute rules and conditional mandatory attribute rules are often associated with each other.

8.3.1.4 Mandatory attribute group rules

Some transactions include groups of attributes of which none are simply mandatory, but at least one of those attributes must be present. The following rules are examples of this:

> Each **Flight Booking Confirmation** must specify a **Mobile Phone No**, an **E-mail Address**, or both.

> Each **Flight Booking Confirmation** must specify a **Credit Card No** or an **Electronic Funds Transfer Payment Receipt** but not both.

> Each **Flight Booking Confirmation** must specify exactly one of the following: a **Postal Address**, an **E-mail Address**, or a **Fax No**.

8.3.1.5 Multi-valued attribute cardinality rules

A multi-valued attribute may be governed by additional cardinality rules defining the minimum and maximum numbers of that attribute that may be present. For example,

> A **Scheduled Flight** must not specify more than 7 **Days of Operation**.

8.3.2   Attribute content rules

This section covers all rules governing what values attributes may have, except uniqueness rules (covered in Section 8.5).

8.3.2.1   Value set rules

Every set selection attribute (see Section 4.7.3) is restricted to values in a defined set. For example,

> The **Travel Class** specified in each **Flight Booking Request** must be First Class, Business Class, Premium Economy Class, or Economy Class.

Other attributes (or combinations of attributes) may also be restricted to values in a defined set. For example, each Australian address should only have a combination of **Locality Name** and **Postal Code** that is recognized by the Australian Post Office. This rule is best modeled as a relationship to a **Locality Postal Code** entity class, as in Figure 64.

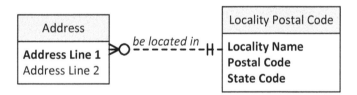

Figure 64: Validating locality data in an address

8.3.2.2   Range rules

A quantifier attribute (see Section 4.7.6) may be restricted to values within a particular range. This may be:

- a minimum, as in

> The **Order Quantity** specified in each **Order Item** must be at least 1.

- a maximum, as in

> The **Temperature** recorded in each **Temperature Reading** must be at most 140°F.

- a minimum and maximum, as in

> The **Number of Passengers** specified in each **Flight Booking Request** must be between 1 and 9 inclusive.

Unlike the above limits on Order Quantity and Number of Passengers, which are **hard limits**, the limit on Temperature quoted above is an example of a **soft limit**. If a customer enters a negative or zero **Order Quantity** or **Number of Passengers**, an error message should be displayed, and the transaction should not proceed to completion until that error is corrected. By contrast, while no temperature reading greater than 140°F has yet been recorded, it is possible that a higher reading could be recorded in the future. In this case, therefore, a warning message should be displayed requesting confirmation of the high reading.

8.3.2.3   Attribute uniqueness

As there are various uniqueness rules governing attributes, relationships, and combinations of attributes and relationships, discussion of these is deferred to Section 8.4.6.

8.3.2.4   Data consistency rules

Two attributes of an entity may be jointly governed by a data consistency rule. Typically one attribute must be either greater than or less than another. This is often true of pairs of dates. For example,

> The **Date of Death** (if any) of a **Person** cannot be earlier than the **Date of Birth** of that **Person**.

> The **Expiry Date** of a **Contract** cannot be earlier than the **Effective Date** of that **Contract**.

> The **Return Date** specified in a **Flight Booking Request** cannot be earlier than the **Departure Date** specified in that **Flight Booking Request**.

Some attributes may be mutually constrained across a related set of entity instances. For example,

> The sum of the **Shares** held by all the **Proprietors** of each **Real Estate Parcel** must equal 1.

Thus, if the values of the **Share** attribute in the **Proprietors** instances related to one **Real Estate Parcel** instance were 1/2, 1/3, and 1/4[78], there is an error, and at least one **Share** must be corrected.

Each derived attribute (see Section 4.3) must be consistent with the attributes from which it is derived. For example, **Range** of a **Vehicle** is **Fuel Tank Capacity** divided by **Fuel Consumption Rate**. If **Fuel Tank Capacity** or **Fuel Consumption Rate** of a **Vehicle** changes, **Range** of that **Vehicle** also changes. If each derived attribute's derivation formula is documented, no rule statement is required.

8.3.2.5 Temporal data rules

The majority of temporal attributes (see Section 4.7.5) are subject to rules, typically to ensure that proposed business activities occur in a sensible sequence, or that there is consistency and data integrity within a set of data representing a long-standing arrangement such as employment.

A **simple temporal data rule** requires that a particular date or time fall within a certain temporal range. For example,

> The **Delivery Date** specified in each **Order** must be no earlier than the date on which that **Order** was raised.

---

[78] Fractions are used rather than percentages, as that is the only way to represent 3 equal shares.

A **temporal data inclusion rule** requires that the time periods specified in a set of records (such as an employee's pay records) do not fall outside some other time period (such as that employee's employment period). For example,

> Each day within the **Time Period** specified in each **Employee Payslip** must be within the **Employment Period** recorded for that **Employee**.

A **temporal data completeness rule** requires that the time periods specified in a set of records (such as an employee's pay records) completely span some other time period (such as that employee's employment period). For example,

> Each day within the **Employment Period** recorded for each **Employee** must be within the **Time Period** specified in exactly one **Employee Payslip** for that **Employee**.

> Each day within the **Employment Period** recorded for each **Employee** must be within the **Time Period** specified in at least one **Department Assignment** for that **Employee**.

A **temporal data non-overlap rule** requires that the time periods specified in multiple instances of the same entity class (such as an employee's leave requests) do not overlap each other. For example,

> The **Time Period** specified in each **Employee Leave Request** must not overlap the **Time Period** specified in any other **Employee Leave Request** for the same **Employee**.

A **day type rule** requires that the date set for some activity be restricted to a working day (typically but not necessarily a weekday other than a public holiday). For example,

> The **Payment Due Date** specified in each **Invoice** must not be a Saturday, Sunday, or public holiday in the jurisdiction in which the **Customer** is located.

8.3.2.6 Spatio-temporal data rules

Timetabling systems, whether for a school, an airline, a railway operator, or a bus company, are subject to rules on what can be included in a proposed timetable. These include rules to ensure that a teacher, aircraft, train, or bus is not specified as:

- being in more than one place at once
- moving at an impossible speed from one location to another
- moving at an unsafe or illegal speed from one location to another.

The first two types of rules are examples of laws of physics, which some commentators consider not to be business rules. You should include them with other business rules since the enterprise and its data are as much constrained by these laws as other laws, regulations, and rules.

How should we ensure that these laws are not violated? In the case of a school timetable, each teacher, in each period of each school day, is either assigned to teach a class or has a free period (so-called)[79]. No teacher will be timetabled to be in more than one place at the same time if we apply the following rule:

> A **Teacher** must not *be assigned to* more than one **Class** in the same **Period**.[80]

Moving at an impossible speed from one location to another used to be prevented (when I was a teacher) by ensuring that (on large campuses) no class assignments in consecutive periods without an intervening break (morning or afternoon recess or lunch) required movement between buildings. However,

---

[79] In reality this is a period in which they create and review lesson plans, mark assignments and/or fulfil administrative duties.

[80] We also require that Periods do not overlap.

that broke down in practice, and some schools now have 5-minute breaks between otherwise back-to-back periods.

There are similar requirements of the data to support the rostering of aircraft, ships, trains, buses, or trucks. These requirements are broadly similar, whatever the mode of transport, so I'll confine myself to a discussion of railway rolling stock rostering. A locomotive or train cannot be rostered to be in more than one place at once, and cannot move between locations at an impossible, unsafe, or illegal speed. The first requirement is met by applying the following rule:

> A **Locomotive** or **Consist** must not *be assigned to* more than one **Roster** at the same time.

The second requirement is met in practice by:

- providing data that defines the minimum duration of a train movement between each pair of timing locations (e.g., stations for passenger trains), either directly or by derivation from distance and maximum speed data; and

- applying the following rules:

> The difference between the **Start Time** and **End Time** of each **Movement** in a **Roster** must not be less than the **Minimum Duration** defined for movements between the **Start Location** and **End Location** of that **Movement**.

> The **Start Location** of the first **Movement** in each **Roster** to which a **Locomotive** or **Consist** may *be assigned* must be the same as the **End Location** of the last **Movement** of the previous **Roster** to which that **Locomotive** or **Consist** may *be assigned*.

8.3.2.7 Attribute format rules

If an attribute has been defined as a temporal attribute (see Section 4.7.5) it must conform to the relevant format rules. For example:

- a **Date** or **Datetime** attribute:
    - must include the day, month, and year in the appropriate sequence for the country of operation (or an agreed sequence for a multinational enterprise operating in countries with different sequences, e.g., the US and the UK)
    - cannot specify a month number outside the range [1,12] or a day number outside the range [1,31] with additional restrictions for those months that have fewer than 31 days[81].

- a **Datetime**, **Time of Day**, **Time of Week**, or **Time of Week of Month** attribute cannot specify a minute outside the range [0,59] or an hour outside the range [0,23] (unless AM and PM suffixes are being used, in which case the hour must be in the range [1,12]).

These rules apply to all temporal attributes and so do not need to be documented in the business information model.

There are other attributes which must comply with format rules, such as:

- phone numbers:
    - these should include only digits (and the '+' sign and parentheses for international numbers)
    - there is either a fixed number of digits or minimum and maximum numbers of digits, depending on the country
    - some websites allow the inclusion of spaces while others do not

- e-mail addresses: the format rules for these are quite complex, and outside the scope of this book[82]

---

[81] The restriction for February depends on whether the year is a leap year or not.

- personal names: given individual creativity and (at least in many countries) no laws governing personal names, I always recommend that enterprises do not specify format rules for any personal names. Unfortunately, there are enterprises whose websites do not allow spaces or apostrophes in a person's surname, even though these are common in many cultures, e.g., von Trier, van de Heide, de Sousa, O'Reilly.

If the proposed application system requires a date to be supplied in some situations, but there is the possibility that some persons may not remember the exact date, consideration should be given to using *partial dates* rather than complete dates. I've discussed previously the possibility that elderly patients may not remember the year they were born (even if they could remember the month and day of month), or may remember the year but not be sure of the month or day. A similar scenario is when employers or health insurers require a detailed record of all serious health-related events such as operations, serious illnesses, etc., going back years. It's all I can do to remember the year, let alone the month and day, so, whenever I've been required to enter a complete date, I've picked a random date within the year I think I had the operation or illness. I suspect that if the enterprise required you to enter the year number but left the month and day numbers optional, it would obtain a more reliable record.

8.3.2.8 Variant and invariant attributes

Some attributes of real-world concepts are **invariant** in that each instance of that concept has a value for that attribute that does not change. For example, each person has only one date of birth, which does not change. By contrast, although each person has only one weight at any given time, that weight (unfortunately!) changes over time.

---

[82] They are listed in the Internet standard RFC5322.

Again there is a difference between **real-world rules** and **data rules**. In the real world, a person's date of birth cannot change but, in the data world, it may have been entered incorrectly and need to be corrected. An attribute that should never change in data is an artificial identifier such as **Customer Number**.

> The **Customer Number** of a **Customer** cannot be updated.

Even with attributes that can legitimately change value, there can be rules on what changes are allowed.

Variant attributes may be subject to **state transition rules**. For example, the possible values of **Marital Status** may be Married, Widowed, Separated, Divorced, Never Married, and Unknown. If the **Marital Status** of a Person is currently Married, Widowed, Separated, or Divorced, updating that **Marital Status** to Never Married should be prevented (except to correct invalid data):

> The **Marital Status** of an **Employee** may be updated to Never Married only if the **Marital Status** that is currently recorded for that **Employee** is Unknown.

Another impossible transition is from Widowed to Divorced. However, a widowed person may be married then divorced between consecutive occasions on which that person's marital status is recorded, so while the following is true in the real world, it is *not* true in the world of data:

> The **Marital Status** of an **Employee** must not be updated to Divorced if the **Marital Status** that is currently recorded for that **Employee** is Widowed.

Variant attributes may be subject to **monotonic transition rules**. For example, an employment agreement may include the rule that the hourly pay rate of an employee must not be decreased. However, I've never encountered such a rule in practice.

8.4   Relationship rules

Some practitioners and commentators I have encountered say that cardinality and optionality are the only business rules governing relationships, some even going so far as to say that relationship cardinality and optionality and mandatory attributes are the only business rules governing any data model. This is far from being the case.

8.4.1   Cardinality and optionality

In Figure 65, the following relationship ends are marked as "optional 1 or more", and are therefore all theoretically unconstrained:

- the number of Subjects a Teacher may teach

- the number of Teachers that may teach a Subject

- the number of Allocations specifying a particular Teacher (although there cannot be more than the number of Periods that Teacher is available, i.e., count(**Available Days of Week**) × the number of Periods per Day)

- the number of Allocations specifying a particular Room (although there cannot be more than the number of Periods in a week, i.e., 5 × the number of Periods per Day)

- the number of Allocations specifying a particular Subject (although the number will in practice be some multiple of the **Number of Lessons per Week**).

All other relationship ends are constrained, either by requiring a minimum of one entity instance (e.g., each **Allocation** must be for exactly one **Subject**) or a maximum of one entity instance (e.g., each **Allocation** must be for at most one **Teacher**). The reason Teachers and Rooms are optional in an Allocation is that the weekly timetable of Lessons for a Subject are planned first, and Rooms and Teachers are then allocated.

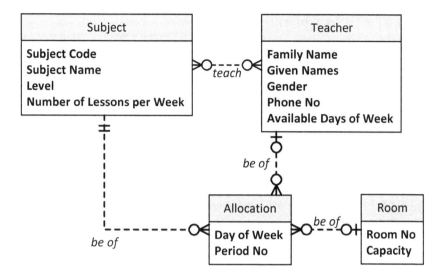

Figure 65: A school timetable

Some relationships are also governed by other rules, as described in subsequent sections.

As with an attribute, a relationship that is mandatory in the real world may be optional in data. For example, every person has exactly two biological parents in the real world but, in the data world, some persons may not know their biological father, and an orphan or adoptee may not know either biological parent.

Again as with each attribute, each end of each relationship has one of three possible cardinalities:

- mandatory in data, e.g.

> Each **Student** must have exactly one **Residential Address**, which must be recorded against that **Student**.

- mandatory in the real world but optional in data, e.g.

> Each **Student** must be *the biological child of* exactly two **Responsible Adults**, which may be omitted from the record of that **Student**.

- optional in the real world, e.g.

> Each **Student** may or may not *play for* a **Team**.

Since data modeling tools only make the distinction between mandatory and optional, I recommend that in your data modeling tool:

- you mark only those relationship ends that are *mandatory in data* as mandatory

- you indicate whether the relationship end is mandatory or optional *in the real world* in either the definition field or some other free text metadata field available in the tool.

The second step may seem like additional effort for no benefit. However, if you don't include that information, automatic generation of statements to describe the model (see Section 10.5.2) would lead to statements like "Each **Student** may or may not be the biological child of exactly two **Responsible Adults**", which reviewers are likely to reject.

8.4.2   Conditional cardinality

Relationships may exhibit **conditional cardinality**. For example, in Australian property law, a **Tenancy** (the ownership of a property) can only be of one of the following types:

- Sole Tenancy: one party has sole ownership of the property

- Joint Tenancy: two or more parties jointly own the property (or share thereof) with the right of survivorship, i.e., if one tenant dies, their interest automatically passes to the remaining joint tenant(s)

- Tenancy in Common: two or more parties own equal or unequal shares in the property.

The relationship between **Tenancy** and **Proprietor** (the legal term for Owner) is therefore:

- 1:1 if the Tenancy Type is Sole Tenancy, but

- 1:n if the Tenancy Type is Joint Tenants or Tenants in Common, with the additional condition that there are at least 2 Proprietors.

This can be modeled in two ways, illustrated in Figure 66 and Figure 67. The simpler model in Figure 66 does not explicitly support the conditional cardinality, which would have to be documented separately.

Each **Tenancy** that is a Sole Tenancy must *be held by* exactly one **Party**, which must be recorded against that **Tenancy**.
Each **Tenancy** that is not a Sole Tenancy must *be held by* two or more **Parties**, which must be recorded against that **Tenancy**.

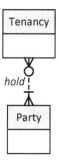

Figure 66: A simple tenancy model

The model in Figure 67 explicitly supports the conditional cardinality and only requires the second rule to be documented.

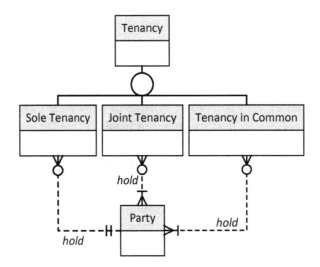

Figure 67: Tenancy subtypes

8.4.3   Mandatory relationship groups

Many enterprises model the various persons and organizations they deal with using a "Party and Role" model, as shown in Figure 68. Most require that a **Party** must play at least one of the listed Roles. In this case, a **Party** is not recorded unless he, she, or it is a **Customer**, **Supplier**, or **Employee**.

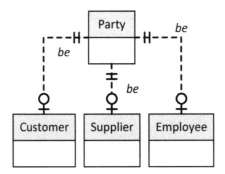

Figure 68: Roles played by Parties

Relationship cardinality does not ensure this. An explicit rule statement must be documented stating this rule:

> Each **Party** must *be* at least one of a **Customer**, **Supplier**, or **Employee**.

8.4.4 Recursive relationships

8.4.4.1 Hierarchies

In a hierarchy, there are rules on which relationship instances can exist. For example, who can report to whom:

- no Employee can report to themself

- if Employee A reports to Employee B, Employee B cannot report to Employee A

- if Employee A reports to Employee B and Employee B reports to Employee C, Employee C cannot report to Employee A

- and so on.

However, we do not have to explicitly document these rules in the business information model since they apply to *all* hierarchies.[83]

Every recursive 1:n relationship I've encountered has been a hierarchy. However, you may one day encounter one that isn't a hierarchy. For this reason, I have always documented each recursive 1:n relationship in a business information model explicitly as a hierarchy, as a cue to apply the appropriate rules during logical data model development.

---

[83] However we will have to consider them in the logical data model, as discussed in Section 11.12.2.

8.4.4.2   Non-homogenous hierarchies

A hierarchy of employees is homogenous, in that every member of the hierarchy is an employee. Non-homogenous hierarchies are those where members of the hierarchy at different levels are known by different generic names (States and Local Government Areas in Australia and Regions in New Zealand), as in Figure 69.

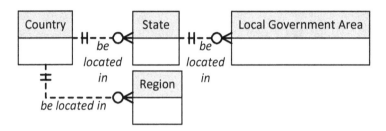

Figure 69: Levels of Australian and New Zealand government

This model enforces these rules:

Each **Local Government Area** must *be located in* exactly one **State**.
Each **State** must *be located in* exactly one **Country**.
Each **Region** must *be located in* exactly one **Country**.

It doesn't enforce these rules:

Each **State** must *be located in* the **Country** Australia.
Each **Region** must *be located in* the **Country** New Zealand.

A single recursive hierarchy, as shown in Figure 70, enforces *none* of these rules.

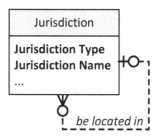

Figure 70: Generic hierarchy of government

The solution is to add a **Jurisdiction Type** entity class, with its own recursive relationship, which includes only allowable combinations of **Jurisdictions**. This takes care of the first three rules but does not manage the other two rules unless we add a **Country** attribute to the **Jurisdiction Type** entity class, as in Figure 71.

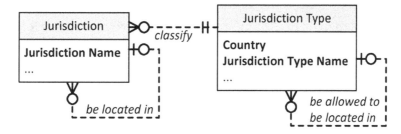

Figure 71: Generic hierarchy of government with rules recorded in data

This is an example of data-driven rules, discussed in Section 8.8.

8.4.4.3 Recursive relationship rules generally

There are many varieties of recursive relationship[84]:

- An **acyclic relationship** is one in which:
    - if A is related to B and B is related to C, C cannot be related to A

---

[84] (Halpin, 2015) refers to the rules governing each type of recursive relationship as **ring constraints**.

- o if A is related to B, B is related to C, and C is related to D, D cannot be related to A
- o and so on.

All hierarchies are acyclic.

> No **Employee** can at the same time *report to* and *manage* (directly or indirectly) the same other **Employee**.

- An **irreflexive relationship** is one in which no entity instance can be related to itself. All hierarchies are irreflexive.

> No **Employee** can *report to* themselves.

- A **reflexive relationship** is one in which every entity instance is related to itself, e.g., every Country permits work by citizens of the Country itself (as well as some other Countries in some cases). With such a relationship, there is no need to record each reflexive instance (e.g., Australia permits work by citizens of Australia). The only instances that need to be recorded are those where a Country permits work by citizens of some other Country (e.g., Australia permits work by citizens of New Zealand). These do not require rule statements.

- There are recursive relationships that are neither reflexive nor irreflexive, e.g., Performers can record tracks written by other Performers and tracks written by themselves, but some Performers only record tracks written by other Performers. These do not require rule statements.

- An **intransitive relationship** is one in which, if A is related to B and B is related to C, A cannot be related to C. All hierarchies are intransitive. However, an additional rule statement is not required for a hierarchy, as intransitivity is a necessary consequence of the relationship being 1:n. Intransitive non-hierarchic relationships rarely occur in business domains, so they are not considered further.

- A **transitive relationship** is one in which A being related to B and B being related to C implies that A is related to C, e.g., **Person** may *be an ancestor of* **Person**. These do not require rule statements.

- There are recursive relationships that are neither transitive nor intransitive, e.g., **Country** may *share a border with* **Country**. These do not require rule statements. Note that this relationship is also irreflexive.

- An **asymmetric relationship** is one in which, if A is related to B, B cannot be related to A. All acyclic relationships are necessarily asymmetric. Relationships that are asymmetric but not acyclic rarely occur in business domains, so they are not considered further.

- A **symmetric relationship** is one in which A being related to B implies that B is related to A, e.g., **Country** may *share a border with* **Country**. These do not require rule statements. However, since the shared border between France and Germany could be recorded either as [France sharing a border with Germany] or [Germany sharing a border with France], a design decision is required: are all shared borders recorded once, or are they all recorded twice? It is important that a "free for all" is not allowed, whereby some are recorded once and others twice.[85] That could yield inconsistent query results if aggregate functions are involved.

- There are recursive relationships that are neither symmetric nor asymmetric, e.g., **Person** may *like* **Person** (as, for example, on Facebook), **Country** may *require a visa from citizens of* **Country**. These do not require rule statements.

---

[85] This can be achieved using a **trigger** as described in Section 11.17.1.

- An **antisymmetric relationship** is one which may include self-referencing instances but not instances that are reflections of other instances. For example, one can teach oneself a skill but, if I teach you a skill, you cannot then teach it to me. However, antisymmetric relationships occur rarely in business domains, so are not considered further.

8.4.5   Quasi-recursive relationship pairs

Two relationships between the same two entity classes are often subject to rules that are analogous to the recursive relationship rules discussed in the previous section.

8.4.5.1   Irreflexive relationship pairs

Figure 72 is a fragment of an airline flight schedule data model. No Australian long-haul airline currently allows you to book a single flight from a Port back to the same Port (as distinct from a return flight from a Port to some other Port then back to the original Port)[86].

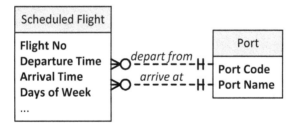

Figure 72: Flight schedule

---

[86] "Round-trip" flights or "joyrides" used to be available, but that was before you could book flights online.

The rule we need here is:

> Each **Scheduled Flight** must *depart from* and *arrive at* different **Ports**.

8.4.5.2 Symmetric relationship pairs

Consider the partial model of a network in Figure 73. Given the possibility of bidirectional Links, a Link between Node A and Node B could be represented as being from Node A to Node B or as being from Node B to Node A.

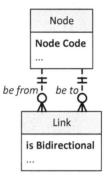

Figure 73: A network model

This raises a design issue. The developers may prefer that each bidirectional Link be recorded twice in the **Link** table, once in one direction and once in the other. While this might make some queries easier to write, it introduces redundancy and requires code to be written that ensures that whenever a Link is inserted, the reverse form of that Link is also inserted.[87]

An arguably better policy is to allow a Link only to be recorded in one direction, which requires a rule. The simplest rule to express (and to code for) relies on this relationship pair also being irreflexive:

> Each **Link** must *be from* and *be to* different **Nodes**.

---

[87] This can be achieved using a **trigger** as described in Section 11.17.1.

All we need is to choose some unique attribute of the entity class at the 1 end of each relationship (it doesn't matter which one) and use a data consistency rule statement involving an inequality:

> The **Node Code** of the **Node** that a **Link** must *be from* must be less than the **Node Code** of the **Node** that that **Link** must *be to*.

8.4.5.3 Acyclic relationship pairs

Bill of Materials data (specifying which Parts form part of sub-assemblies and ultimately products) is necessarily acyclic:

> No **Part** can at the same time *form part of* and *consist of* (directly or indirectly) the same other **Part**.

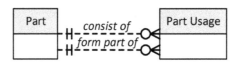

Figure 74: Bill of Materials

8.4.6   Non-transferable relationships

Figure 75 is a fragment of a railway rolling stock scheduling data model. A Multiple Unit can be reallocated from one Depot to another in terms of maintenance responsibility, but a Track can't be. The relationship between **Multiple Unit** and **Depot** is **transferable**, whereas the relationship between **Track** and **Depot** is **non-transferable**. We don't need a rule statement for the transferable relationship, but we do need one for the non-transferable relationship:

> A **Track** cannot be moved from one **Depot** to another.

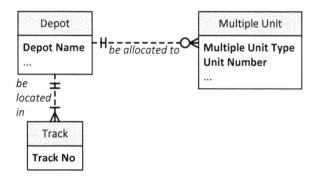

Figure 75: Rolling stock depot allocation

What about n:n relationships? Consider Figure 76. If an Employee is reassigned from one Project to another, is that a reassignment or the ending of one assignment and the start of another? Actually, this is less the concern of the data modeler as it is the concern of users (who will expect to record assignments to Project in an intuitive manner) and developers (who will, of course, build a system that meets users' needs).

Figure 76: Employee Project assignments

8.5   Uniqueness rules

A well-designed system should prevent inadvertent errors by those entering transaction data, be they customers or employees. For example:

- an order taking system should warn a customer if they have ordered the same product more than once in the same order:

> Each **Order Item** that may *be included in* the same **Order** must *specify* a different **Product**.

- an online flight booking or travel insurance system should reject the same combination of person name and birth date appearing more than once:

> Each combination of **Person Name** and **Birth Date** of an **Insured Traveler** that is to *be covered by* the same **Travel Insurance Request** must be different.

Uniqueness rules also need to be defined for master data. For example, no two Customers should be assigned the same Customer No:

> Each **Customer** must have a different **Customer No**.

Sometimes no one attribute is unique, but two or more attributes must have a different combination of values for each entity instance. For example, some railway operators allocate numbers to Multiple Units[88] starting from 1 for each type of unit, so that unit numbers alone aren't unique. In this case, the railway rolling stock database would include the following uniqueness rule:

> Each **Multiple Unit** must have a different combination of **Unit Type Code** and **Unit No**.

Multi-valued attributes are also generally governed by uniqueness rules. For example, the **Days of Operation** and **Meal Services** attributes of a **Scheduled Flight** should not include repeated days or meals:

> Each of the **Days of Operation** of a **Scheduled Flight** must be different.

This rule, plus the fact that there are only seven possible values for **Day of Operation**, means that the rule stated in Section 8.3.1.5 is actually redundant. It is quite common for one or more rules to prevent another rule from being violated.

---

[88] A Multiple Unit is a permanently-coupled self-propelled passenger-carrying rolling stock consist.

8.6   Documenting data rules

This section discusses where to record data rules in the data modeling tool (if possible) rather than how to present them to business stakeholders for review, which is discussed in Section 10.5.2.

8.6.1   Documenting attribute rules

This section covers documentation of all rules governing attributes except uniqueness rules, which are covered in Section 8.6.3.

8.6.1.1   Documenting mandatory attributes

All data modeling tools that I have used support the marking of attributes as mandatory. This facility should be used to document mandatory attributes.

8.6.1.2   Documenting other single-attribute rules

If your data modeling tool provides a free text metadata field for recording the rules on each attribute (or a multi-purpose free text metadata field in addition to the attribute definition field), that is the place to document all other attribute business rules. For example, the attributes of **Multiple Unit Type**, listed in Section 7.5.2, are subject to the rules listed in Figure 77.

Attribute	Data type	Mandatory?	Data rules
Unit Type Code	unit type code	Yes	
Number of Cars	count	Yes	must be > 0
Seated Capacity	count	Yes	must be > 0
Outline Gauge	outline gauge	Yes	must be one of 'N', 'M', 'E', 'W'
Propulsion	propulsion	Yes	must be one of 'Diesel', 'Electric'
Transmission Type	transmission type	No	must be one of 'Hydraulic', 'Mechanical', 'Electric' if and only if **Propulsion** is 'Diesel'
Axle Load	weight	Yes	must be > 0
Unit Length	length	Yes	must be > 0
Unit Weight	weight	Yes	must be > 0
Speed Band	speed band	Yes	must be a speed band defined in the Train Operating Manual
Uniqueness rules			Each **Multiple Unit Type** must have a different **Unit Type Code**

Figure 77: Attribute rule documentation

Each data rule can then be used in the following template

- "The <attribute name> of each <entity class name> <data rule>.", e.g.

> The **Axle Load** of each **Multiple Unit Type** must be > 0.

The uniqueness rules are separated out since some uniqueness rules operate over multiple attributes (see Section 8.6.3).

8.6.1.3   Documenting data consistency rules

A data consistency rule (discussed in Section 8.3.2.4) may govern:

- a pair of attributes, e.g., **Expiry Date** and **Effective Date**
- an aggregate function on one attribute across a related set of entity instances, e.g., the sum of the **Shares** held by the **Proprietors** of a **Real Estate Parcel**.

A data consistency rule governing a pair of attributes should be documented against one of those attributes with a statement that references the other attribute.

A data consistency rule governing an aggregate function of a single attribute should be documented against that attribute.

8.6.1.4   Where to document attribute rules

If your data modeling tool does not provide a separate field for recording data rules governing attributes, they can be appended to the attribute definition or recorded in a separate document.

8.6.2   Documenting relationship rules

This section covers documentation of all rules governing relationships except uniqueness rules, which are covered in Section 8.6.3.

8.6.2.1   Relationship markings in a data model diagram

All data modeling tools support the marking of relationship lines to indicate cardinality and optionality, and a few support marking relationships as transferable. Others support the marking of relationships as **identifying**, but that is not relevant in a business information model, although it is relevant in a logical data model (discussed in Section 11.8.1).

8.6.2.2   Other relationship rules

Few (if any) data modeling tools provide free text metadata fields for recording other rules on relationships or even multi-purpose free-text metadata fields that can be used for that purpose. Moreover, the only one I've ever encountered that provided that functionality did not provide any easy means of documenting rules governing multiple relationships, such as:

- mandatory relationship groups (see Section 8.4.3)
- irreflexive relationship pairs (see Section 8.4.5).

Given the above, **conditional cardinality** of a relationship (see Section 8.4.2) may need to be documented against one of the related entity classes rather than the relationship.

The best place to document a **mandatory relationship group** is in a suitable free-text metadata field describing the common entity class, e.g., **Party** in the case of "Each **Party** must *be* at least one of a **Customer**, **Supplier**, or **Employee**."

Each **irreflexive relationship pair** should be documented in a suitable free-text metadata field describing *one* of the involved entity classes. That entity class should be the one that is at the "more than one" rather than the "one" end of each relationship. For example, "Each **Scheduled Flight** must *depart from* and *arrive at* different **Ports**." should be documented against **Scheduled Flight** (see Figure 72 in Section 8.4.5).

If a recursive relationship represents a hierarchy (see Section 8.4.4.1), all you need to do is state that it is hierarchic. If your data modeling tool provides a free text metadata field for describing relationships, use that, otherwise use a free text metadata field associated with the related entity class.

If a recursive relationship represents something other than a hierarchy, document the characteristics of the relationship (acyclic, irreflexive, reflexive, intransitive, transitive, asymmetric, symmetric, and/or antisymmetric—as described in Section 8.4.4.3) in a suitable free text metadata field describing either the relationship or the related entity class.

8.6.2.3   Where to document relationship rules

To summarize the above discussion:

- cardinality and optionality should be indicated using the standard symbols at each end of each relationship

- conditional cardinality should be documented as a complete rule statement in either (a) a free text metadata field (if any) describing either the relationship or the related entity class, or (b) a separate document

- mandatory relationship groups and irreflexive relationship pairs should be documented as complete rule statements in either (a) a free text metadata field describing one of the related entity classes (if any), or (b) a separate document

- recursive relationships should either (a) be categorized as described in Section 8.4.4.3 in a free text metadata field (if any) describing either the relationship or the related entity class, or (b) documented as complete rule statements in a separate document

- transferability should be indicated using (a) the relationship marking supported by the data modeling tool (if any), (b) a free text metadata field describing the relationship (if any), (c) a free text metadata field describing one of the related entity classes (if any), or (d) a complete rule statement in a separate document.

If a separate document is used to record any data rules, it should be used to record *all* data rules except perhaps mandatory attributes and relationship cardinality and optionality.

8.6.3 Documenting uniqueness rules

A uniqueness rule may govern:

- one single-valued attribute, e.g.

Each **Customer** must have a different **Customer No.**

- one multi-valued attribute, e.g.

Each of the **Days of Operation** of a **Scheduled Flight** must be different.

- multiple attributes, e.g.

Each **Multiple Unit** must have a different combination of **Unit Type Code** and **Unit No.**

- multiple relationships, e.g.

Each **Order Item** that may *be included in* the same **Order** must specify a different **Product.**

- a combination of attributes and relationships, e.g., (in Figure 78)

Each combination of **Person Name** and **Birth Date** of an **Insured Traveler** that is to *be covered by* the same **Travel Insurance Request** must be different.

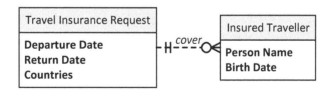

Figure 78: Travel Insurance Request

I'm not aware of any data modeling tool that supports the documentation of *all* these types of uniqueness rule. Therefore, each uniqueness rule should be documented as a complete rule statement against the appropriate entity class:

- the entity class whose name appears immediately before "must be different" in rule statements that end with the phrase "must be different"

- the entity class whose name appears immediately after "Each" in other rule statements.

8.7   Decision rules

Decision rules govern how business processes respond to particular events. For example:

- based on data provided by an applicant for a loan, a process will either approve a loan or reject the application

- the fee to be charged by a bank at the end of a month in connection with an account may depend on a number of factors such as the minimum balance that month, the number of years the account holder has been a customer, and so on

- the number of points earned for a flight taken by a member of a frequent flier program depends on

  - the Travel Class (e.g., First, Business, Economy)
  - the Fare Class (e.g., Fully Refundable, Non-refundable Advance Purchase)
  - the Membership Level (e.g., Platinum, Gold, Silver)
  - the flight distance.

These rules are best managed as **data-driven rules**, discussed in the next section.

8.8 Data-driven rules

Decision rules are, by their nature, data-driven. We have also seen (in Figure 56 in Section 6.8 and Figure 71 in Section 8.4.4.2) how an entity class holding allowable combinations can be used to govern a generalized hierarchy.

8.8.1 Rule volatility

Rules that are likely to change over time can also benefit by being controlled by updateable data rather than being "locked in" to data structure or process code. Some rules are more likely to change than others, as illustrated in Table 1.

Type of Rule	Example	Volatility
Laws of nature: violation would give rise to a logical contradiction	A person can be working in no more than one location at a given time	Zero
Legislation or international or national standards for the industry or business area	Each customer has only one Social Security Number	Low
Generally accepted practice in the industry or business area	An invoice is raised against the customer who ordered the goods delivered	Low
Established practice (formal procedure) within the organization	Reorder points for a product are centrally determined rather than being set by warehouses	Medium
Discretionary practices: "the way it's done at the moment"	Stock levels are checked weekly	High

Table 1: Rule volatility

8.8.2 Decision support data

The data that supports such rules should be modeled in the business information model, as that data will be visible to those business users who will manage that data, and their managers. Figure 79 illustrates typical data to support loan approvals, for which the decision criteria may change over time.

Loan Approval Decision
Loan Purpose Minimum Loan Amount Maximum Loan Amount Minimum Repayment Period Maximum Repayment Period **Customer Credit Rating** **is to be Approved** Rejection Reason

Figure 79: Loan approval decision support data

This data includes:

- **criterion attributes** (**Loan Purpose** to **Customer Credit Rating** inclusive)
- a **decision attribute** (**is to be Approved**), and
- a **decision reason attribute** (**Rejection Reason**, which is only relevant in those instances where **is to be Approved** is False).

There are two types of criterion attribute:

- Set selection attributes, such as **Loan Purpose** and **Customer Credit Rating**, allow for different decisions to be taken for each possible combination of Purpose and Credit Rating.
- Minimum and maximum pairs, such as **Minimum Loan Amount** and **Maximum Loan Amount**, allow the same set of decisions to be made for a range of loan amounts. For example, different sets of decisions might be made for loans less than $10,000, loans between $10,000 and $50,000, and loans over $50,000.

Some criterion attributes are optional. This is because, for some values of **Customer Credit Rating**, no approval can be given whatever the loan purpose, amount, or repayment period. Only a single instance of the decision data is required for each such value of **Customer Credit Rating**, with all other criterion attributes being null. There may be other criteria that are irrelevant to the decision for certain situations, e.g., for Loans below a certain amount to be repaid in 12 months, the Purpose is irrelevant.

Figure 80 illustrates typical data to support account fee decisions, which may change over time, with five criterion attributes and one decision attribute (**Fee Amount**).

Account Fee Decision
Account Type
Last Month Minimum Balance
Minimum Account Age
Maximum Account Age
Customer Category
Fee Amount

Figure 80: Account fee decision support data

Figure 81 illustrates typical data to support frequent flier points earning decisions, which may change over time, with five criterion attributes and one decision attribute (**Number of Points**).

Points Earning Decision
Travel Class
Fare Class
Minimum Flight Distance
Maximum Flight Distance
Membership Level
Number of Points

Figure 81: Frequent Flier points earning decision support data

8.8.3   Rules that vary according to location or situation

These should also be supported by data. For example, when planning travel, any multi-stage itinerary suggested by a website can be assumed to be feasible and take into account transit times at hubs. For air travel, the minimum transit time at a hub depends on:

- whether arrival and departure are at the same terminals
- at large airports, the arrival and departure gates
- whether the transit involves entry into or exit from a country, in which case a worst-case estimate of the time taken to get through customs and immigration will have to be included.

Figure 82 is a model of the data used to estimate transit times. **Immigration Duration** and **Emigration Duration** are optional as they only apply to international airports.

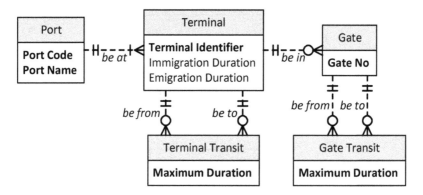

Figure 82: Airport transit

8.8.4   Making sure that other data complies with rule data

Note that when we include rule data in a model, this takes the place of explicit rule statements, and this can create a problem. I once reviewed a data model that included plenty of rule data, which was endorsed by business stakeholders. When the resulting system was demonstrated, a user entered some rule data and then tried to enter master data that violated the rules just entered. The master data was accepted by the system without any error message.

It turned out that no one had told the developers that master data must comply with the rule data.

If you include rule data in a model, *make sure that the process specification includes the validating of other data against the rule data*.

8.9   Pre- and post-event rules

There is one more thing we need to consider with respect to rules. A timetabling application is one in which the data precedes the events it represents. All rules that ensure a feasible and safe timetable should be applied to timetable data as it is being entered.

Application systems that record data about events after they have happened need to allow the recording of data that violates rules, since (as the saying goes) "rules are made to be broken" in the real world. For example, an application system that manages planning applications for new buildings in a city should enforce rules that govern which building types and usages are permitted in which zones. However, if that application system is also used to record details of existing buildings, it must allow for non-compliant building data to be recorded.

8.10   Summary

The data modeler must analyze and document all data rules and decision rules, in either the business information model or the logical data model.

Each attribute may be governed by rules, including:

- whether it is mandatory (required in all instances), conditionally mandatory (required in specific instances), prohibited in specific instances, or belongs to a group in which exactly one or at least one must be specified

- what values it may take, in terms of a valid value set, range, or consistency (in comparison with some other attribute or the same attribute in other instances)

- its format

- whether it may be updated.

Each relationship is governed by rules, including:

- its cardinality and optionality (including conditional cardinality and belonging to a group in which exactly one or at least one must be specified)

- whether it is transferable.

Recursive relationships and quasi-recursive relationship pairs are governed by additional rules.

Uniqueness rules (which require each instance to be different) may cover one or more attributes, relationships, or combinations thereof.

How and where you document rules depends on the data modeling tool you are using. Mandatory attributes and relationship cardinality and optionally are supported by all tools. Other rules may be included in metadata, appended to attribute or entity definitions, or recorded in a separate document.

Additional data should be added to the business information model to support any decision rules or other data-driven rules.

If you include rule data in a model, make sure that the process specification includes validating other data against the rule data.

Pre- and post-event rules require different error handling.

Chapter 9.   Features of a business information model

A **business information model** describes the design of a data resource in such a way as to be readily understood by business stakeholders. In particular, a business information model:

- models the enterprise's information requirements rather than a particular database solution

- names all entity classes, attributes, and relationships using business terminology rather than IT terminology, cryptic names, or abbreviations not in common use

- includes only those data items visible to users, and excludes non-visible identifiers, foreign keys, internal audit data, system control data, etc.

- is normalized: it does not include redundant copies of attributes in other entity classes (sometimes added to logical data models for performance reasons)

- may, however, include derived or calculated attributes that have business significance, e.g., an **is Current** attribute derived from **Effective Date** and **Expiry Date**, or a **Total Order Amount** calculated from **Order Line Quantities** and **Unit Prices**.

To meet these criteria, a business data model uses a richer language (one which expresses more with less) than might be used in a logical data model. The principal techniques are:

- depicting n:n relationships as such, rather than breaking them down into intersection entity classes and pairs of 1:n relationships (which is only one way to implement n:n relationships), except when those relationships have attributes

- depicting supertype/subtype taxonomies as such, without any indication as to how these might be implemented

- depicting each classification (e.g., **Gender**) as a **set selection attribute**[89], rather than a relationship to a "type table" with **Code** and **Meaning** attributes (which is not the only way to implement classifications)

- representing objects with composite internal structure as "black boxes" (i.e., single attributes), in particular:

  o marking **composite attributes**[90] (e.g., person names, phone numbers, addresses, quantities with variable units, **Start Date/End Date** pairs) as composite and documenting the structures of such attributes elsewhere in the model, rather than listing all their sub-attributes

  o marking **multi-valued attributes**[91] (e.g., the **Meals Served** and **Days of Operation** for an international flight) as multi-valued, rather than adding **dependent entity classes** for such attributes

- instead of modeling the structures (such as "version tables") required to manage history, marking attributes for which a history of changes is to be recorded

- instead of modeling time-variant 1:n relationships as n:n relationships, leaving them as 1:n and indicating whether a history of changes is to be recorded

- using attribute classes rather than DBMS data types to classify attributes in terms of the behavior of the represented real-world property.

---

[89] See Section 4.7.3.
[90] See Section 4.4.
[91] See Section 4.5.

9.1 What should a business information model include?

A business information model should include:

- all concepts in scope, depicted as entity classes and named using business terminology

- all business-visible attributes in each of those concepts, named using business terminology, including:

  - composite attributes as such, rather than broken down into simple attributes
  - multi-valued attributes as such, rather than being moved into a separate entity class (unless they are coupled, as described in Section 4.5.1)
  - set selection attributes as such, rather than as relationships to category entity classes
  - any derived attributes of business significance

- supertype/subtype hierarchies using a distinct subtyping notation, rather than relationships

- all business-relevant relationships between the concepts in scope, including:

  - n:n relationships as such, rather than being represented by an intersection entity class (other than those with attributes)
  - any derived relationships of business significance

- the attribute class of each attribute

- if there is a requirement for change history to be recorded, marking of time-variant attributes and relationships, rather than creating additional data structures to manage time-variance

- documentation of data rules[92], decision rules[93], and data-driven rules[94].

---

[92] See Section 8.6.

9.2   What should a business information model not include?

A business information model should not include any of the following:

- non-visible identifiers (those columns with names typically ending in **ID**)
- foreign keys[95]
- data structures to support time variance
- non-visible data such as audit data or system control data
- cryptic or abbreviated entity class names or attribute names
- DBMS data types.

However, these may be appropriate to include in a *logical data model*.

9.3   Isn't that just a conceptual data model?

There are many different published definitions of the term **conceptual data model**, and many published models labeled as conceptual data models vary significantly in what has been included and excluded.

For example, among the published definitions one can find the following statements:

- with respect to whether attributes should be included in a conceptual data model:
    - o   "entity class … and its … attributes" in one
    - o   "attributes are usually not added" in another
    - o   "no or extremely limited number of attributes" in yet another

---

[93] See Section 8.7.
[94] See Section 8.8.
[95] If the data modeling tool includes foreign keys anyway, they should be hidden.

- with respect to whether optionality of a relationship should be marked in a conceptual data model:
  - "optionality … [is] omitted" in one
  - "may or may not include cardinality and nullability" in two others.

Data models published online and labeled as conceptual data models include:

- models with no attributes at all, models with primary keys but not foreign keys, and models with both primary and foreign keys

- models with classification attributes and models with "type tables".

Given this state of affairs, I recommend that practitioners do not use the term **conceptual data model**, as to do so would risk confusing any recipient of something labeled as such.

9.4   Summary

A **business information model** must be readily understood by business stakeholders, so must:

- model all information requirements, using business terminology, rather than a database solution

- include all business-visible data items and only them

- *not* show primary or foreign keys

- depict n:n relationships, supertype/subtype taxonomies, classifications, and composite objects as such rather than as how they might be implemented

- *not* model time-variance by adding version tables or using n:n relationships to represent time-variant 1:n relationships

- model attribute behavior using attribute classes rather than DBMS data types.

A logical data model should include primary and foreign keys, data structures to support time-variance, non-visible data, and DBMS data types.

The term **conceptual data model** is ill-defined, so is unsuitable for use.

— Part 2 —

From requirements to an application system fit for purpose

Chapter 10. Developing a business information model

This chapter describes the process of developing a business information model as defined in Part 1.

10.1   Getting started

There are some important things to establish before developing a business information model:

- What is the purpose of the model? As we saw in Section 1.6.1, this might be:
    - to form part of the design of a new application or data resource
    - to document an undocumented existing application or data resource that is to be modified or be the source of a data migration
    - to provide a framework for system integration
    - to provide an enterprise-wide understanding of the enterprise's data.

- If the model is for a new application or data resource, what development methodology is to be used?

- What resources exist to identify the concepts to be included in the model?

- What data modeling tools are already in use?

How we proceed will depend on the answers to those questions.

If the purpose of the model is to provide a framework for integration or an enterprise-wide understanding of the enterprise's data, a taxonomic glossary (as described in Section 7.4.2) may be sufficient. If business stakeholders expect to see a data model diagram, a business information model with only entity classes and relationships (i.e., without attributes or business rules) *may* be sufficient.

If designing a new application or data resource, or documenting an existing application, a complete business information model (entity classes, attributes, relationships, and business rules) will be required.

Moreover, if designing a new application or data resource, the development methodology affects how we proceed. In particular, an Agile project will develop a data model incrementally, and the required concepts will emerge from the process. This generally means that the principal source of data concepts is the knowledge of those business stakeholders embedded in the project. I discuss how to manage data modeling in an Agile project in Section 10.4.1.

Finally, if no data modeling tools are currently installed within the enterprise, and more than just a taxonomic glossary is needed (see above), you will need to select a data modeling tool, as described in Section 10.2. Otherwise, you can move directly to Section 10.3.

10.2   Selecting a data modeling tool

Many enterprises quite reasonably don't see themselves as being in the business of software development, preferring instead to purchase commercial off-the-shelf software. If you need to develop a data model for such an enterprise, I recommend you ignore the relatively expensive enterprise tools. Given their cost, a separate tool selection project would be required, which would involve (a) identifying and agreeing on tool functionality requirements, (b) shortlisting candidate tools against those requirements, and (c) thoroughly reviewing the shortlisted tools' requirements fit, one-off and ongoing costs, vendor service levels, etc.

There are, however, some freeware and open-source data modeling tools. Not having used any, I shan't name any. Instead, I've set out below a checklist of required functionality. Beware of tools that are marketed as data modeling tools but which are actually database management tools with diagramming functionality added. This is because many of these are only suitable for **reverse engineering** (producing a diagram of an existing database) rather than producing a data model from which a database design can be developed.

If you are unsuccessful in finding a suitable tool, Section 10.2.2 suggests an alternative.

10.2.1   What tool functionality is required?

Essentially a data modeling tool should enable you to:

- produce data model diagrams that are easy for business stakeholders to understand

- record metadata about entity classes, attributes, and relationships, including definitions and business rules

- automatically generate scripts with which to build a database corresponding to the data model

- produce reports setting out all relevant information about each data model (to be viewed on-screen or printed as required).

10.2.1.1 Diagramming functionality

The following functionality is *essential* for effective development and presentation of data models:

- support for the "crow's foot" relationship notation used throughout this book and arguably the most intuitive

- support for subtype hierarchies, using connecting lines that are clearly distinguishable from those representing relationships

- support for both business information models and logical data models as described in this book, which includes:

  - the ability to display entity classes without primary keys (these are neither required nor appropriate in a business information model) and, as a consequence, to draw relationships without foreign key attributes being displayed
  - the ability to mark primary keys and foreign keys in logical data models
  - the ability to present any diagram without any of the logical/physical metadata that generally appears in UML diagrams

- user control of the positioning of entity class boxes and relationship lines, and the survival of that positioning after saving, closing, and reopening of a diagram

- automatic prevention of lines passing behind boxes[96]

- easy prevention of relationship lines crossing (unless the model can't be depicted without crossing lines)

- support for **subject areas**[97], with the ability for some entity classes to be assigned to multiple subject areas.

---

[96] There was once a popular UML tool that would draw association lines that crossed behind object class boxes, which was very confusing.

The following functionality is *desirable*:

- the ability to display only one name per relationship even if named in both directions

- automation of transformations, including:

  - inclusion of a foreign key column or columns to represent each 1:n relationship (see Section 11.8.1)
  - replacement of an n:n relationship by an intersection entity class and two 1:n relationships (see Section 5.9.1 and Section 11.8.4)
  - rolling up subtype attributes into the supertype (see Section 11.11)
  - moving a set of attributes into another entity class during normalization (see Section 4.2)
  - adding version tables to handle time-variance (see Section 11.12)

- support for UML notation (if required)

- marking attributes and relationships as derived, or allowing non-alphabetic characters in attribute and relationship names (see Sections 4.3 and 5.8)

- support for composite and multi-valued attributes (see Sections 4.4 and 4.5)

- the ability to add text or graphics to the data model diagram (see Section 5.6).

10.2.1.2 Metadata functionality

The following metadata functionality is required:

- attribute metadata:

  - name, definition (essential)

---

[97] A **subject area** is a subset of a data model representing a specific function performed by the enterprise.

- o   data type: DBMS or user-defined (essential)

- relationship metadata:

   - o   name in each direction (essential)
   - o   cardinality and optionality at each end (essential)
   - o   whether the relationship is transferable (desirable)
   - o   whether the relationship is an **identifying relationship**[98] (only in a logical data model) (desirable)
   - o   a free text field for other data rules (highly desirable)
   - o   marking whether historical instances of a relationship are required (only in a business information model) (desirable)

- user-defined data types (possibly labeled as domains) (highly desirable)

- data rule markings:

   - o   mandatory attributes (essential)
   - o   primary and foreign keys (logical data model only) (essential)
   - o   uniqueness rules on single or multiple attributes (desirable)
   - o   a free text field for other data rules (desirable)
   - o   marking whether a history of changes in an attribute's value is required (only in a business information model) (desirable).

10.2.1.3   Reporting functionality

The following reporting functionality is required:

- automatic generation from a logical data model of **DDL** (**Data Definition Language**), which specifies the structure of a relational database (essential)

- data model reports, in which entity classes, attributes, and relationships can be listed, along with relevant metadata (essential)

- such reports to be user-customizable (highly desirable)

---

[98] See Sections 11.8.1 and 11.8.4.

- automatic generation of relationship sentences from entity class and relationship names (desirable)

- export of metadata to a word processor or spreadsheet (essential).

The facility to export metadata to a spreadsheet enables a comprehensive standardized verbal description of the data model (as described in Section 10.5.2) to be easily generated.

10.2.2   Alternative tooling

I have, on more than one occasion, successfully developed useful data models for enterprises without a data modeling tool, by using Office products (an Excel workbook, Word documents, and Visio diagrams). This requires more effort in actual model development (and ensuring consistency) than if you were using a data modeling tool. However, this can be offset against the effort of selecting, installing, and learning to use such a tool.

10.3   Sourcing data requirements

There are various ways to source the data to be included in a business information model:

- a **requirements specification** (if one exists)

- workshops with business stakeholders

- interactions with business stakeholders during **Sprints** in an **Agile** project

- specifications of proposed user interfaces

- the actual user interface and database of an undocumented existing application.

10.3.1   Requirements specifications

If a requirements specification exists, it should be your initial source. A good requirements specification consists of a set of individual requirements, each documented in business language and each individually identified.

However, like many other human activities, there are more people doing it than doing it well. Requirements specifications are generally produced by Business Analysts. If the Business Analyst has an understanding of (a) the business, (b) the issues it needs to manage, and (c) the problems it needs to solve, there is a good chance that they can produce a requirements specification from which data requirements can easily be inferred. Requirements analysis is a professional activity drawing on specialized skills, which needs an entire book—such as (Hay, 2003)—to cover adequately.

However, I have encountered people who seem to think a Business Analyst can move from industry to industry and immediately start producing requirements specifications while ignorant of each industry's terminology and business drivers.

Even if the Business Analyst has understood what business stakeholders have told them, they can still produce a requirements specification from which a data model is more difficult to develop. I have frequently encountered different terms in a requirements specification that turn out to be synonyms (e.g., Customer and Client, or Train and Consist). This can be manageable if two different requirements, one using one term and one using another, turn out to be alternative statements of the same requirement. However, if the two requirements conflict, the data modeler is faced with the task of establishing which one is correct. In this situation, office politics can come into play. Often the data modeler is part of the IT project team, who may not have been granted direct access to business stakeholders, so the data modeler has to convince the

Business Analyst to go back to the business stakeholders to seek clarification. Unless handled diplomatically, this may not proceed smoothly.

Another problem that you might encounter in a requirements specification is the presence of homonyms (the same term having multiple meanings). Where these exist, but the Business Analyst hasn't noticed, there is a potential for confusion.

Another issue—this one being relatively easy to deal with—is the issue of instantiation. This is where multiple variants of a generic requirement are separately specified, each with subtly different wording, and not necessarily consecutively, rather than being specified once. If the data modeler has a good memory, they may realize that there is only one requirement.

Finally, be aware that explicit requirements often imply other requirements which have not been explicitly stated. For example, one requirements specification I worked from made no mention of any requirement for historical data. By chance, I was chatting with the developer building the reports to be generated by the proposed system, and I noticed he had a different requirements specification from the one I was working with. This turned out to be the *reporting* requirements specification. The project manager had seen no reason for me to have it. This was because—as everyone knows—a report can only include data that is in the database, so he concluded that no additional data requirements could be inferred from the reporting requirements. Not so! A cursory glance at the reporting requirements revealed that many reports included month-on-month or year-on-year comparisons. As the system was being developed to manage a volatile real-world situation, I ended up having to add historical data to almost every entity class. As I've stated in Section 5.5, the business information model merely needs a marking against those attributes for which a historical record is required. The actual data structures in which history is recorded are added in the logical data model (see Section 11.12).

10.3.2 Workshops

Successful workshops are those in which participants can speak freely about what is important to the enterprise, what they would do better if they could, what they would do if they were able, what problems they face in their work that could be overcome with a better system, what data they need for decision making, etc.

There are many mistakes that might derail a workshop, but two are particularly dangerous:

1. The facilitator may try to control business stakeholder conversations. This can take two forms:

    o   One is to assume that business stakeholders think like data modelers, as in "today we're going to decide what entity classes there should be in the data model". This is guaranteed to dampen any enthusiasm to contribute.
    o   The other is to decide without advising the business stakeholders that the focus is going to be on a particular type of data model artifact and disallow any contributions that aren't of that type. I actually once witnessed a junior modeler who was doing really well eliciting entity classes from participants. We had Customer and Product and Order and Invoice up on the board, then someone said "Delivery Date". The modeler's reply was "that's not an entity" which caused *all* business stakeholders to resist making further contributions. Even the arrival of refreshments didn't restore the momentum.

2. We used to capture what was being said onto a whiteboard and then photocopy it. That's still not a bad idea, but it's now more common for someone to type what is being said into a laptop that is being projected onto a screen visible to all, thus avoiding double handling. Whatever you do, ***don't*** try to enter the findings into a data modeling tool, or your audience will quickly lose interest. Type everything verbatim into a word processor document or a spreadsheet. Use one document paragraph or spreadsheet cell for each contribution, ideally (if

participants agree) with the initials of the contributor in case you need to get back to them for clarification. All you need is a touch typist who can spell. Don't even aim for complete sentences during the workshop. Afterward, you can edit a little before sending the notes to all participants, with a covering e-mail asking them to confirm the notes as an accurate record or advise of anything not correctly captured. As a bonus, this often elicits further useful information to be factored into the data model.

10.4   Developing the model

10.4.1   Data modeling in an Agile project

There is a belief that Agile projects don't need data modelers, apparently because the data model a) has no independent value, and b) can be derived from the user interface design. However, on more than one occasion, I have been called in to rescue an Agile project that was having trouble refactoring and integrating the various data structures they were generating. I was also once called in to support remedial work on an application system developed by an Agile project, which was now exhibiting more and more errors due to misunderstanding of the underlying data.

Having developed data models in many Agile projects, I would say that the data modeler in an Agile project must:

- embrace the idea that the data model will evolve and change throughout the project

- participate as a fully-involved team member in all sprints

- create an initial data model in **Sprint 0** based on the **user stories** developed in that Sprint; ideally, this should be done by (a) developing a business information model, (b) sharing it with the rest of the project team, (c) incorporating any feedback, then (d) creating from that model a logical data model (as described in Section 11.2)

- by the end of each **Sprint**, have updated the data model to be ready for the next Sprint; this should be done by (a) updating the business information model, then (b) replicating each business information model change in the logical data model (as described in Section 11.16).

Finally, they must be prepared to respond rapidly but thoughtfully to each request for a change to the data model. That doesn't necessarily mean executing each change exactly as requested, but instead deciding how best to adapt the model to meet the requirement that has prompted the request. For example, if the request is for an additional object class (entity class), they should consider whether there is an existing object class that can support the requirement, with or without modification. They must explain their decision and be prepared to adapt it if other team members provide convincing evidence for something different. I cover the management of data model change in Section 10.4.5.

10.4.2   Data modeling in other projects

One apparent reason for the view that Agile projects don't need data models or modelers is the mistaken perception that, in a **waterfall project**, the data model is created and signed off before any development starts and is then "set in stone", never to be changed. I started data modeling in the 90s and was a developer before that. In all that time, I can't recall a data model that didn't change over the course of the development project. As a result, I developed a technique for managing data model change, which I'll describe in Section 10.4.5.

10.4.3   Building the initial model

The various sources of data requirements will yield a "grab bag" of useful (and not so useful) candidate entity classes, attributes, and relationships. I find the following procedure helps me to quickly move from that situation to an initial model to be shared with the team.

For each candidate entity class identified:

- confirm that it is required

- add the entity class to the model

- identify candidate attributes of this entity class

- once all candidate attributes have been identified, then for each attribute:
    - confirm that it is required
    - if it is not required, delete it, otherwise
    - establish whether it belongs in this entity class or another (see discussion on **functional dependency** in Section 4.2.1)
    - if it belongs in another entity class,
        - identify which other attributes also belong to the other entity class
        - add the other entity class to the model (if it is not already present)
        - add a 1:n relationship between the original and new entity classes (with cardinality 1 at the new entity class end)
        - move the non-unique attribute and the other attributes that depend on it to the other entity class
    - write a definition for the attribute
    - identify what business rules govern the attribute

- identify candidate relationships involving this entity class

- once all candidate relationships have been identified, then for each relationship:
    - confirm that it is required
    - if it is not required, delete it, otherwise
    - identify the associated entity classes
    - identify the cardinality and optionality at each end
    - choose an appropriate verb phrase in each direction
    - document the business rules that govern this relationship.

10.4.4   Documenting assumptions and questions

During sourcing data requirements and building the initial model, it is inevitable that you will make various assumptions about the data. You need to be aware of when you're making an assumption, and document each assumption immediately before you move on, otherwise the assumption can easily become an apparent fact. All assumptions should be checked with business stakeholders before becoming enshrined in the model. Similar questions will occur to you during this process. Unless you can't proceed without knowing the answer to a question, it is better to (a) document questions as they arise, then (b) arrange a meeting with business stakeholders to get the answers to all the questions that have arisen.

I use a single word processor document for both assumptions and questions, with two sections (one headed Assumptions and another headed Questions), with a two-column table in each. In the left-hand column is a description of an assumption or the wording of a question, with the right-hand column left blank for verification or rejection of each assumption and an answer to each question.

10.4.5   Managing data model change

Various types of change might be required to a data model. Many changes are quite local. For example, none of the following should affect any other attributes of the same entity class, let alone any other entity classes:

- adding an attribute to an entity class
- changing the data type of an existing attribute
- changing the business rules governing an existing attribute
- marking an existing invariant attribute as variant or vice versa.

However, some changes can affect artifacts other than the one being changed. Some examples of this appear in the following sections.

10.4.5.1 Renaming an entity class or attribute

If an entity class needs to be renamed, first ask why. If it's just that the entity class isn't currently named using the preferred term, check where else the current entity class name is used in other entity classes and attributes. For example, if the **Customer** entity class is to be renamed to **Client**, there may be another entity class named **Customer Account**, which should probably be renamed to **Client Account**. There may be attributes of the **Customer** entity class named **Customer No** and **Customer Name**, which should probably be renamed to **Client No** and **Client Name**. The term Customer may also have been used in definitions, relationship names, and/or business rules, so it should probably be replaced by Client in each case.

However, the renaming may signify a semantic change. For example, in a human resources system, there may be a requirement to rename the **Employee** entity class to **Human Resource**. This may just be a rebadging of the Employee concept with no semantic implications: the same people are represented by the renamed entity class as were represented before the rename. Alternatively, the rename may reflect the inclusion of contractors for which different data may be required. As another example, in a rail operations system there may be a requirement to rename the **Locomotive** entity class to **Motive Power Unit**. This broadens the scope of the entity class, since multiple units (permanently-coupled self-propelled passenger-carrying consists) would be covered by that term but not by the term **Locomotive**. Are more attributes required, e.g., **Seated Capacity**? Is there already a **Multiple Unit** entity class? If so, rather than the suggested rename:

- a new **Motive Power Unit** entity class should be created, and
- **Locomotive** and **Multiple Unit** be made subtypes of **Motive Power Unit**. This is dealt with in more detail in Section 10.4.5.3.

10.4.5.2 Moving an attribute between entity classes

There are two main reasons to move an attribute between entity classes:

1. It can be moved from an entity class representing a complex event, activity, or arrangement (e.g., **Order**) to a related entity class representing some detail of that event, activity, or arrangement (in this case **Order Item**). For example, **Delivery Address** might be moved from **Order** to **Order Item** to allow customers to order goods for different recipients in the same Order. On the other hand, if that flexibility is *not* required and **Delivery Address** is already in **Order Item**, it should be moved to **Order**.

2. It can be moved from a subtype to a supertype or vice versa. For example, in Figure 41 in Section 6.1, **Propulsion Type** is an attribute in four out of the five subtypes of **Road Vehicle** (**Trailer** being the exception). It could therefore be moved to **Road Vehicle** as an *optional* attribute (even though mandatory in each subtype) and business rules added to state that **Propulsion Type** is mandatory for all Road Vehicles except Trailers and must be absent for Trailers.

Whatever the reason, whenever an attribute is moved between entity classes, the following should be checked to see if any rewording is required:

- the attribute's definition and any business rules

- any references to the attribute in any other attribute's definition or business rules.

10.4.5.3 Generalizing

There are various changes that might be categorized as generalization:

- A supertype might be added over some existing entity classes that then become subtypes of that supertype. For example, if **Person** and **Organization** had previously been separate entity classes, a **Party** supertype could be added, and **Person** and **Organization** made subtypes of **Party**. This would require the following consequential changes:

o Each attribute common to all the existing entity classes should be moved from those entity classes into the supertype, where it should be made optional unless mandatory in *all* existing entity classes. Note that the existing attribute names may not be the same, in which case a new common name would be needed (as depicted in Figure 83).

o Each relationship common to all the existing entity classes should be moved from those entity classes to the supertype, where it should be made optional at the other end unless mandatory at the other end for *all* existing entity classes. Note that the existing relationship names may not be the same, in which case a new common name would be needed.

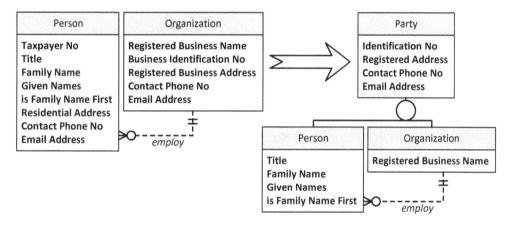

Figure 83: Making Person and Organization subtypes of Party

• An attribute might be added to a supertype. If this happens, check whether the attribute applies to *all* subtypes of that supertype and would be mandatory for *all* of those subtypes. If an attribute does not apply to at least one subtype, or applies to all subtypes but would not be mandatory for at least one subtype, it must be made optional.

• A relationship might be added to a supertype. If this happens, check whether the relationship applies to *all* subtypes of that supertype and would be mandatory at the other end for *all* of those subtypes. If a relationship does not apply to at least one subtype, or applies to all subtypes but would not be mandatory at the other end for at least one subtype, it must be made optional at the other end.

- A new subtype might be added to a supertype. If this happens, check whether all attributes and relationships of the supertype apply to the new subtype. If an attribute does not apply to the new subtype, it must either
  - o be made optional (if not already)—as depicted in Figure 84—and a business rule added stating that it must be absent for supertype instances associated with the new subtype, or
  - o be moved to each of the existing subtypes of the supertype—as depicted in Figure 85.

If a relationship does not apply to the new subtype, it must either
  - o be made optional at the other end (if not already)—as depicted in Figure 84—and a business rule added stating that it must be absent for supertype instances associated with the new subtype, or
  - o be moved to each of the existing subtypes of the supertype—as depicted in Figure 85.

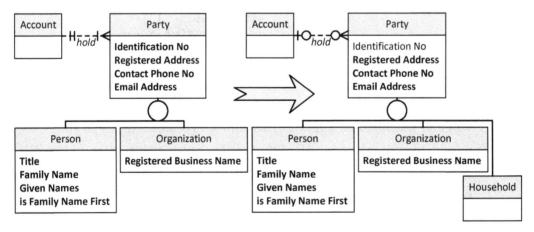

Figure 84: Adding a new subtype to a supertype (option 1)

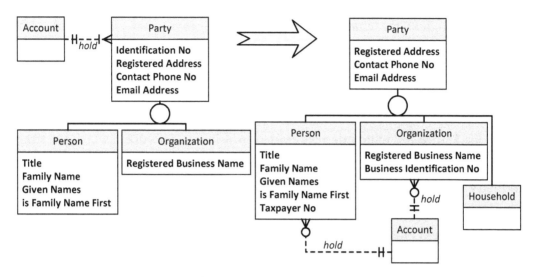

Figure 85: Adding a new subtype to a supertype (option 2)

10.4.5.4 Documenting changes

Before making any change to a data model, I recommend that you:

- list all the changes you intend to make, including the individual steps for each complex change

- make sure you have identified all other changes that need to be made, either for consistency or as a consequence

- make sure there are no conflicting changes, and

- sort the list into a logical sequence.

This allows you to make all changes confidently and, when necessary, interrupt the process of change and be able to pick up where you left off.

It also allows you to provide developers and business stakeholders with a list of all changes made. This is particularly important for anyone tasked with reviewing the original model: reviewers can check that their feedback has been incorporated and, where there is more than one review cycle, reviewers of the second and subsequent versions who have also reviewed the previous version can focus on just the changes. The list of changes should also include any changes requested but ***not*** made, with reasons.

10.4.6   Alternative models of the same reality

Consider Figure 86, which depicts part of a railway network. Data for a train control application system needs to include a model of the track layout. The industry standard for such models uses the concepts of Nodes and Links. In this part of the network there are 11 Nodes, each denoted by a black dot, with identifiers based on the code for the station followed by the Node Suffix:

- WMD1, PTA1, PTAA, GVL1 on the line from West to East, and
- GVL2, GVLB, PTAB, PTA2 and WMD2 on the line from East to West.

Each section of track between two adjacent Nodes is recorded as a Link, e.g., WMD1-PTA1 (but not WMD1-PTAA). Most Links are unidirectional: trains can only legitimately travel in the direction shown by an arrow symbol. However a train travelling from the West can negotiate the crossover from PTAA to PTAB to reach GVL3 via GVLB. It can then return to the West via GVLB, PTAB and PTA2. Links PTAB-GVLB and GVLB-GVL3, on which trains can legitimately travel in both directions, are therefore bidirectional.

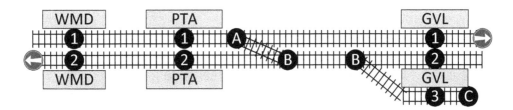

Figure 86: Fragment of a railway network

What would the data model look like? A train control system needs to know (among other things) which Nodes are joined by Links and whether those Links are unidirectional or bidirectional, as modeled in Figure 87. However there is another way to model this, depicted in Figure 88. With this model, a bidirectional Link is represented as two Links between the same two Nodes, one in one direction and one in the other.

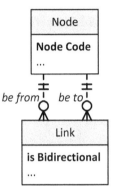

Figure 87: One rail network model

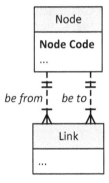

Figure 88: An alternative rail network model

An important additional requirement is that impossible movements are prevented. A train must not be timetabled to move from PTAA to PTA2 via PTAB, nor from GVL2 to GVL3 via GVLB. For safety's sake we also want to prevent movements from GVL1 to PTAB via PTAA (a movement from GVL1 to PTAB is a "wrong way" movement which may occur in an emergency). There are many ways this can be modeled:

1. add an entity class representing all impossible movements as pairs of Links (in this case PTAA-PTAB|PTAB-PTA2, GVL2-GVLB|GVLB-GVL3, and GVL1-PTAA|PTAA-PTAB)

2. add an entity class representing all impossible movements as triplets of Nodes (in this case PTAA|PTAB|PTA2, GVL2|GVLB|GVL3, and GVL1|PTAA|PTAB)

3. add an entity class representing all *possible* movements as pairs of Links

4. add an entity class representing all *possible* movements as triplets of Nodes.

Figure 89 and Figure 90 depict options 1 and 2 respectively.

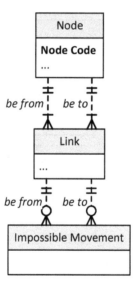

Figure 89: One impossible movement model

In summary, there may be more than one way to model the same reality. If there are alternative possible models, it pays to evaluate the advantages and disadvantages of each. Which model would be easiest to program for? Which model would be easiest to source data for?

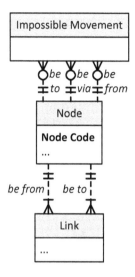

Figure 90: Another impossible movement model

10.5   Communicating the model

The whole point of a business information model is to allow business stakeholders to review our modeling decisions before investing effort in developing a logical data model, implementing the model in a relational database or other platform, and developing code based on the model. If the business stakeholders are to review the model effectively and comprehensively, it must be presented in an understandable format.

10.5.1   Data model diagrams

Contrary to popular opinion, a data model diagram is not the most effective means of communicating a model to anyone who needs to understand it in its entirety. For a start, no diagram is going to be able to depict all modeling decisions such as data types and business rules without becoming so cluttered that the reviewer would not know where to start. The reviewer inevitably has to refer to accompanying textual documentation containing entity class and attribute definitions and business rules.

Secondly, a diagram is two-dimensional so, unless the reviewer is organized and disciplined, there is a risk of missing something on the diagram. I once encountered a business stakeholder who was methodically ticking each entity class name, attribute name, and relationship line end as he went. He was even able to take a break every so often and restart his review precisely where he left off. But I only ever saw that once.

In Section 10.5.2, I shall discuss a tried and tested technique for describing a data model verbally, reducing reliance on the diagram. However, diagrams are still useful for conveying the big picture, so I shall first offer some suggestions on how to present data model diagrams.

10.5.1.1 Subject areas

If a model includes ten or more entity classes, consider breaking it up into **subject areas**. For example:

- divide a data model for a mail-order system into separate diagrams for the ordering, payment, and dispatch functions
- divide a data model for a human resources system into separate diagrams for the recruitment, training, payroll, and other functions
- divide a data model for a train control system into separate diagrams for network geography, timetable, rolling stock assignment, and actual train movements.

This will inevitably lead to the same entity classes appearing in more than one subject area. For example, in a data model for a human resources system, **Employee** will inevitably appear in most (if not all) subject areas.

10.5.1.2 Sharing and presentation

When you share any data model diagrams with business stakeholders, do not assume that they understand the meanings of the symbols and markings that are used. Always provide a legend explaining all symbols and markings, such as Figure 2 in Section 1.9 of this book. This is particularly important if you circulate the model to stakeholders via e-mail before (or instead of) presenting it.

I have successfully used two techniques in presenting a model to stakeholders:

1. Build up a model (or subject area) from a single entity class, adding other entity classes and connecting relationships a few at a time. This allows stakeholders to focus on one thing at a time, and allows the model presenter to guide them on the journey of understanding. Rather than using the data modeling tool to do this and risk displaying the diagrams out of sequence, I prefer to output the various diagrams to a PowerPoint presentation and check them for logical flow before presenting. If your data modeling tool supports subject areas, you can create a subject area for each step of the build-up.

2. Give the entity class boxes in each complete subject area (not those created for the purpose of building up) a different background color. This appears to improve understanding. Those entity classes that appear in multiple subject areas should be assigned a "home" subject area and be given the color representing that subject area in all subject areas. For example, when presenting the data model for a copyright and royalties management system, I used pink for the **Authors** subject area (covering all data about authors and their rights). However, in the **Payments** subject area (covering payments to authors), for which green was used, the box representing the **Author** entity class was pink. Be sure to use pastel shades with a black font (or dark colors with a white font) so that the entity class and attribute names are easily read.

10.5.2   Describing the model verbally

In 2001, I was responsible for designing a database to support environmental monitoring by a water authority. The data model was quite complex, and I realized that it was unreasonable to expect business stakeholders to review it thoroughly using only diagrams and accompanying documentation. In those days, I was using a data model management tool I had built in Microsoft Access (with diagrams produced in Microsoft Visio) to support the many clients who had no data modeling tool. As an experiment, I modified the tool to generate a series of statements describing the model. These were numbered for identification, and each had an empty box beside it in which a reviewer could place a tick (to signify agreement), a cross (to signify disagreement), or a question mark (to signify that they were not sure).

These responses enabled my colleagues and me to rapidly fix errors in our understanding of the client's requirements. Where question marks had appeared, we renamed the relevant data model artifacts or changed their definitions to improve mutual understanding. This method of review worked so well that many reviewers no longer bothered with the diagrams.

In April 2002, I presented my findings (under the title "Assertion-based Modeling") at the DAMA International Conference in San Antonio, Texas, where I received much positive feedback. I used the term **assertion** because the statements were not so much statements of fact as assertions of what we believed to be the case.

I was further encouraged when, in 2003, I read some articles by Terry Halpin for the Business Rule Community, in which he described his approach to generating statements to describe an ORM model. I included a comprehensive set of assertion templates in (Simsion & Witt, 2004) but have subsequently come to realize that a somewhat simpler approach was preferable.

10.5.2.1 Assertion templates

In the assertion templates that follow:

- < and > are used around placeholders for which the nominated items can be substituted

- { and } are used to denote sets of alternative wordings separated by the | symbol, e.g., {A | An} indicates that either 'A' or 'An' may be used. Which alternative is used may depend on

    - o the context, e.g., 'A' or 'An' is chosen to correspond to the term that follows, or
    - o a property of the component being described, e.g., 'must' or 'may' is chosen depending on the optionality of the relationship being described

- … indicates that the preceding placeholder may be repeated as many times as required

- to make templates easier to read, "entity" and "verb" are used rather than "entity class" and "verb phrase".

Each template is followed by an example, which should make these conventions clear.

10.5.2.2 Entity class assertions

For each entity class that *is not* a subtype of some other entity class:

- Each <entity name> is a <definition>.

> Each **Outbound Communication** is any communication from the enterprise to another party to provide or request information or request payment.

For each entity class that *is* a subtype of some other entity class:

- Each <subtype name> is a type of <supertype name> that is <definition>.

> Each **Invoice** is a type of **Outbound Communication** that is a request to a customer for payment for goods or services obtained by that customer from the enterprise.

10.5.2.3 Attribute assertions

For each attribute that is mandatory in data (see Section 8.3.1):

- The <attribute name> of each <entity name > {is | are}[99] <definition>.

- Each <entity name> has {a | an | }[100] <attribute name>, which must be recorded against that <entity name>.

The **Customer No** of each **Customer** is the number assigned to that customer by the enterprise to identify that customer.
Each **Customer** has a **Customer No**, which must be recorded against that **Customer**.

For each attribute that is mandatory in the real world but optional in data:

- The <attribute name> of each <entity name> {is | are} <definition>.

- Each <entity name> has {a | an | } <attribute name>, which may be omitted from the record of that <entity name>.

The **Birth Date** of each **Employee** is the date on which that employee was born.
Each **Employee** has a **Birth Date**, which may be omitted from the record of that **Employee**.

For each attribute that is optional in the real world:

- The <attribute name> (if any) of each <entity name> {is | are} <definition>.

- Each <entity name> may or may not have {a | an | } <attribute name>.

The **Meals** (if any) of each **Scheduled Flight** are the meals and/or refreshments served on that flight.
Each **Scheduled Flight** may or may not have **Meals**.

---

[99] Use "is" for a single-valued attribute, "are" for a multi-valued attribute.
[100] Use 'a' or 'an' for a single-valued attribute, omit for a multi-valued attribute.

10.5.2.4 Relationship assertions

For each relationship end that is mandatory in data (see Section 8.4.1):

- Each <entity 1 name> must <relationship verb> {exactly one | one or more} <entity 2 name>, which must be recorded against that <entity 1 name>.

> Each **Scheduled Flight** must *be from* exactly one **Port**, which must be recorded against that **Scheduled Flight**.

For each relationship end that is mandatory in the real world but optional in data:

- Each <entity 1 name> must <relationship verb> {exactly one | one or more} <entity 2 name>, which may be omitted from the record of that <entity 1 name>.

> Each **Student** must *be the biological child of* exactly one **Father**, which may be omitted from the record of that **Student**.

For each relationship end that is optional in the real world:

- Each <entity 1 name> may or may not <relationship verb> {exactly one | one or more} <entity 2 name>.

> Each **Employee** may or may not *be assigned to* one or more **Projects**.

For each mandatory relationship group (see Section 8.4.3):

- Each <entity 1 name> must <relationship verb> at least one of {a | an} <entity 2 name>, …, or <entity n name>.

> Each **Party** must *be* at least one of a **Customer**, **Supplier**, or **Employee**.

10.5.2.5 Attribute rule assertions

For each attribute rule (other than a mandatory attribute rule) governing each mandatory attribute:

- The <attribute name> of each <entity name> <business rule stub>.

> The **Number of Cars** of each **Multiple Unit Type** must be > 1.

For each attribute rule governing each optional attribute:

- The <attribute name> (if any) of each <entity name> <business rule stub>.

> The **Transmission Type** (if any) of each **Multiple Unit Type** must be one of 'Hydraulic', 'Mechanical', or 'Electric' if and only if **Propulsion** is 'Diesel'.

The business rule stub is what I recommended be documented for attributes as illustrated in Section 8.6.1. For example, "must be > 1".

For each invariant attribute:

- The <attribute name> {(if any)|} of {a|an} <entity name> cannot be updated.

> The **Customer Number** of a **Customer** cannot be updated.

10.5.2.6 Relationship rule assertions

For each hierarchy relationship:

- No <entity name> can at the same time <relationship verb> and <relationship reverse verb> (directly or indirectly) the same other <entity name>.

- No <entity name> can <relationship verb> {themself|itself}[101].

> No **Organization Unit** can at the same time *include* and *be included in* (directly or indirectly) the same other **Organization Unit**.
>
> No **Organization Unit** can *include* itself.

For each irreflexive relationship pair (see Section 8.4.5.1):

- Each <entity 1 name> must <relationship 1 verb> and <relationship 2 verb> different <entity 2 plural name>.

> Each **Redirection Order** must *be from* and *be to* different **Addresses**.

---

[101] Use "themself" for an entity class representing persons, "itself" otherwise.

For each non-transferable relationship (see Section 8.4.6):

- {A|An} <entity 1 name> cannot be moved from one <entity 2 name> to another.

> An **Order Item** cannot be moved from one **Order** to another.

10.5.2.7 Uniqueness rule assertions

For each single-attribute uniqueness rule documented using data modeling tool functionality:

- Each <entity name> must have a different <attribute name>.

> Each **Order** must have a different **Order No**.

For each uniqueness rule governing a multi-valued attribute that is documented using data modeling tool functionality:

- Each of the <attribute name> of {a|an} <entity name> must be different.

> Each of the **Meals** of a **Scheduled Flight** must be different.

For each uniqueness rule governing multiple attributes that is documented using data modeling tool functionality:

- Each <entity name> must have a different combination of <attribute 1 name>, … and <attribute n name>.

> Each **Vehicle** must have a different combination of **State Code** and **Registration No**.

For each uniqueness rule governing multiple relationships that is documented using data modeling tool functionality:

- Each <entity 1 name> that {must|may} <relationship 1 verb> the same <entity 2 name> must <relationship 1 verb> a different <entity 3 name>.

> Each **Order Item** that may *be included in* the same **Order** must *specify* a different **Product**.

For each uniqueness rule governing a combination of attributes and relationships that is documented using data modeling tool functionality:

- Each {<attribute name>|combination of <attribute 1 name>, … and <attribute n name>} of {a|an} <entity 1 name> that is to <relationship verb> the same <entity 2 name> must be different.

> Each combination of **Person Name** and **Birth Date** of an **Insured Traveler** that is to *be covered by* the same **Travel Insurance Request** must be different.

For each uniqueness rule documented with an explicit rule statement:

- <rule statement>

10.6   Summary

Development of a business information model should follow an orderly progression, whether in an Agile or traditional project.

Before starting, the purpose of the model, the development methodology, and sources of data requirements should be identified and agreed upon.

If no data modeling tool is currently in use, either use the functionality list provided in Section 10.2.1 to select a tool or document the model using Office products.

Requirements specifications and workshops are both useful means of sourcing data requirements, but require careful treatment.

In an Agile or traditional project, the data model will inevitably change throughout the project, so it is important to manage data model change carefully.

Any assumptions or questions to business stakeholders should be documented during the modeling process.

Communicating the model clearly is important if the business stakeholders are to review the model effectively and comprehensively. While diagrams are useful in providing a high-level overview, a verbal description of the model using standard statement types is the best way to communicate the detail of a model.

Chapter 11. Modeling stored data: logical data models

A **logical data model** is only required if the intended implementation platform is a **relational DBMS** (traditional or **SQL:2003**-compliant) or an **object-relational DBMS**. A different approach is required if the data resource is to be implemented in **XML**, which is covered in Chapter 12.

Developers are the principal users of a logical data model. If they are programming directly against a relational database, they will think in terms of **tables** and **columns**. If they are using an object-oriented programming environment, they will think in terms of **object classes** and **attributes**. In this chapter, I use the terms "table" (to include "object class") and "column" (to include "attribute").

The process of creating a logical data model from a business information model is fairly straightforward:

1. complete the capture, analysis, and review of data rules
2. make a copy of the business information model
3. remove derived data items
4. rename tables and columns to conform to the naming standard in force
5. add primary keys
6. check normalization
7. handle columns
8. handle relationships

9. handle composite and multi-valued attributes

10. handle supertypes and subtypes

11. handle history recording (if required)

12. handle data rules.

11.1   Completing data rule capture, analysis, and review

If data rules have not all been captured and documented in the business information model, all remaining data rules should be captured, analyzed, added to the business information model (as described in Chapter 8), and reviewed, before preceding further.

11.2   Generating a logical data model from a business information model

The logical data model can be developed by performing well-defined transformations on the business information model. However, the business information model needs to be preserved. This is because, if requirements change during or after the development project, it is the business information model that should be changed first and reviewed, after which the logical data model can be updated to reflect the business information model changes. This process is described in Section 11.16.

Thus, the first step in developing the logical data model is to create a *copy* of the business information model, with each entity class becoming a table and each attribute becoming a column. Most (if not all) data modeling tools support this process and allow for different styles (or levels) of data model. Be aware that some tools I've encountered use the terms "logical data model" for something more like a business information model and "physical data model" for something more like a logical data model.

11.3   Removing derived data items

Any derived data items in the business information model (i.e., any columns representing derived attributes and any derived relationships) should now be removed from the logical data model. This is because derived data should not be stored but derived "on the fly". If it turns out that such derivations are time-consuming, **materialized views** (see Section 11.15.1) can be created to store derived data under DBMS control.

11.4   Naming tables

Most enterprises have naming standards for database tables. These almost always require that there be no spaces in a table name. This is because references to a table with a name containing spaces need to be enclosed in square brackets in SQL and other code.

Just removing the spaces from a multi-word entity class name makes it less easy to read, so one convention commonly used is **Camel case**, either with or without an initial upper case letter. For example, the entity class name **Leave Application** becomes **LeaveApplication** or **leaveApplication**.

Alternatively, an underscore character can replace each space, thus **Leave_Application**.

A further option with either of these conventions is to prefix all table names with either **t** or **t_**, thus **tLeaveApplication**, or **t_Leave_Application**.

11.5   Naming columns

Again, most enterprises have naming standards for database columns. As with table names, there should be no spaces, so again there is the choice of Camel Case or underscore characters.

In some standards, each column name should end with a **classword** which reflects the attribute class of the attribute on which it is based. For many attribute classes, that classword has already been used in the business information model (see Section 7.2) with the following exceptions:

- Boolean attributes in the business information model should be renamed by removing the initial **is** and adding the classword **Flag** or **Indicator**, e.g., **is Family Name First** becomes **FamilyNameFirstFlag** or **Family_Name_First_Flag**.

- Count attributes in the business information model that have been given names starting with **Number of** should be renamed by removing the initial **Number of** and adding the classword **Count**, e.g., **Number of Axles** becomes **AxleCount** or **Axle_Count**.

- **Date and Time** attributes in the business information model should be renamed by removing **and** to use the classword **DateTime**.

Other naming standards mandate the use of prefixes rather than classwords, in what is known as **Hungarian notation**. Some examples of these prefixes are

- **b**, meaning Boolean, e.g., **bFamilyNameFirst**
- **c**, meaning count, e.g., **cAxles**.

11.6 Adding primary keys

Every table must include one or more columns to act as the **primary key**[102]. There are two essential criteria for the primary key column(s):

---

[102] The **primary key** of a table is the **column** (or combination of columns) in that table that holds a unique value (or combination of values) in each **row** of that table, enabling other tables to hold unambiguous references (**foreign keys**) to individual rows.

1. They must be mandatory, meaning every table row must have values for every column making up the primary key.

2. They must be unique, meaning each row must have a different value (or combination of values) in the primary key column(s).

A further criterion is not essential but is highly desirable:

3. They must be stable or non-volatile, meaning the values of the column(s) in each table row should not change over time.

The reason for this third criterion is that, if relationships are implemented using foreign keys (copies of primary key values: see Section 11.8.1), the following must occur whenever a primary key value changes:

- access to all tables with foreign key references to the table with the primary key to be updated must be blocked

- the foreign key constraint (see Section 11.17.1.1) in the database must be dropped

- not only must the primary key be updated, but every matching foreign key must be updated to the new primary key value

- the foreign key constraint must be restored

- access to the blocked tables must be restored.

In a large database, all this could take some time.

11.6.1   Using business information model attributes

While **natural identifiers** (or **business identifiers**) such as names (e.g., **Customer Name, Locality Name, Country Name**) are usually applicable to all instances, they are rarely guaranteed to be unique, and some aren't guaranteed to be stable. By contrast, **artificial identifiers** are by design applicable to all instances and can generally be guaranteed to be unique. This is true whether they are (a) created by an external authority (e.g., **Airport Code, Country Code, Taxpayer Identification**

No), (b) by a nominated authority within the enterprise (e.g., **Product Code**, **Flight No**), or (c) automatically by a system (e.g., **Customer No**, **Order No**, **Account No**). Moreover, most are completely stable (never change over time). Those that do change do so only rarely and only as part of a controlled and publicized process. For example, New York's John F Kennedy Airport (with code JFK) had previously been coded IDL (Idlewild).

While artificial identifiers can generally be guaranteed to be unique, they may only be unique within a limited scope. For example, vehicle registration numbers are only unique within a single state (in the US or Australia), so that **Vehicle Registration Number** can't be used alone as a primary key. However, it can be used in conjunction with **State Code**, the combination being unique. Another example of a multi-attribute primary key appears in Figure 99 in Section 11.10.1.

This ability to include multiple columns in a primary key can create problems for the novice data modeler. I once reviewed a data model in which there was a table of Postal Codes. In Australia, one Postal Code can cover multiple neighboring localities with different Locality Names and the same Locality Name can occur in multiple States, so the data modeler had rightly made **Postal Code** and **Locality Name** the primary key. By analogy, he had then created a table of Countries and made **Country Code** and **Country Name** the primary key. This would have created a significant risk for data quality, as it would have been possible to create multiple entries with the same **Country Code** and multiple entries with the same **Country Name**. The lesson from this is *never include more columns in a primary key than are necessary for uniqueness.*

11.6.2   Adding non-visible primary keys

If a table has a column (or set of columns) that is mandatory, unique, and stable, mark that column or columns as the primary key.

If it doesn't, add a mandatory unique column that won't be visible to users (often referred to as a **surrogate key**). The conventional name for such columns is the table name followed by **ID**, e.g., **EmployeeID** or **Employee_ID**. You should also do this if the enterprise mandates that *all* tables must have a surrogate key.

11.6.3   Adding primary keys: a summary

If the enterprise does *not* mandate that all tables must have a surrogate primary key *and* there is a single column or combination of columns that (a) is applicable to all instances of the table, (b) has a different value or combination of values for each row of the table, and (c) has values that never change (or change only rarely and in well-defined circumstances), make that column or combination of columns (all of which should be mandatory) the primary key. In all other cases, add a mandatory column with a name formed from the table name followed by **ID** and make that column the primary key.

11.7   Handling columns

11.7.1   Choosing DBMS data types

Relational and object-relational DBMSs each provide a number of built-in data types, although they vary from product to product. The data types provided each belong to one of the following categories:

- **numeric**, both fixed-point (exact) and floating-point (approximate)
- **string**, holding strings of characters from a defined set, both fixed length (char) and variable length (varchar[103])

---

[103] In Oracle, varchar2 has superseded varchar.

- **temporal**, holding dates and/or times
- **large**, holding documents, images, or recordings
- **identifier**, holding unique row identifiers.

Object-relational DBMSs and SQL:2003-compliant DBMSs support **user-defined data types**, which can be defined in terms of the above **base data types**. If you are developing a logical data model for use in one of these DBMSs, (a) create a user-defined data type for each attribute class used based on the DBMS data type defined in the appropriate section below, and (b) assign to the column representing each attribute the user-defined data type created for that attribute's attribute class.

11.7.1.1 Columns representing identifier attributes

Whether natural or artificial, visible identifiers should be assigned a string data type, even if those identifiers are currently only numeric, in case alphanumeric identifiers are required later. Use char rather than varchar.

Added surrogate keys should be assigned an identifier data type[104] if available, or one of the integer data types if not. Some DBMSs do not provide specific integer data types but instead provide a number data type that can be specified as having no fractional digits ("decimal places").

If you are assigning an integer or number data type, ensure that you specify enough bits, bytes, or digits to accommodate the maximum number of instances of the entity class that might be expected over the life of the system.

---

[104] DB2 and Oracle include a rowid data type.

11.7.1.2 Columns representing Boolean attributes

As I write this, no DBMS yet provides a Boolean data type, so assign the shortest integer data type available[105] and store the values 1 for true or 0 for false, to allow for Boolean arithmetic[106].

11.7.1.3 Columns representing set selection attributes

Traditionally each set selection attribute has been implemented as a foreign key to a table, holding the available values both as codes and meanings. For example, a Gender table might hold 'F' and 'Female' in the **Code** and **Meaning** columns in one row and 'M' and 'Male' in another row. This was for two main reasons:

1. Holding only 1-character codes rather than 6-character meanings in other tables saved on the amount of storage required.

2. Data entry of just the code rather than the meaning in full required fewer keystrokes.

Storage is no longer the issue that it was and, since drop-down lists are now the norm for such data items, saving keystrokes is not an issue.

Where the number of allowed values is small, it is now more common to use a varchar column with a **constraint** limiting that column to the allowed values (see Section 11.17.1.1).

Only if the number of allowed values is large or there is a requirement for changes to the set of allowed values should a "**type table**" be added. That table should be given the same name as the set selection attribute. It should include a

---

[105] In most DBMSs, this is smallint (2 bytes). In SQL Server this is tinyint (1 byte).
[106] If three-valued logic (see Section 4.7.2) is required, unknown is represented by the absence of a value, i.e. null. This requires that the column be optional rather than mandatory.

column named for the set selection attribute (e.g., **Country Code**) with data type char, along with a **Meaning** column with data type varchar. It should be given a primary key: either the **Code** column or (if and only if the enterprise standard mandates it) a surrogate key (see Section 11.6.2). The set selection attribute should be replaced by a foreign key (see Section 11.8.1), replicating that primary key.

Be aware that any table can be updated by users unless explicitly prevented. Updating of a type table by users should be prevented if (a) there is program logic that depends on one or more values of the set selection attribute (e.g., different logic depending on the **Payment Type** selected), or (b) there is no business requirement for update by users.

If, instead of a type table, a **constraint** is used to limit the column to the prescribed allowed values, this can generally only be changed by a database administrator.

11.7.1.4   Columns representing descriptor attributes

Each of these should be assigned a varchar data type.

11.7.1.5   Columns representing temporal attributes

The DBMS data types to be assigned to these are as follows:

- **Datetime**: use the datetime or timestamp data type, whichever is provided: this may or may not provide time zone and/or daylight saving support[107]
- **Date**: use the date data type
- **Year No**: use the smallint data type

---

[107] For example, SQL Server provides datetime2 (without time zone support) and datetimeoffset (with time zone support).

- **Day of Week**: use the shortest integer data type available (to allow for comparisons and arithmetic), and add a constraint to limit the column to the values 1–7 or 0–6

- **Time of Day**: use
  - the time data type if available[108]
  - the interval day to second data type (in Oracle), or
  - an integer data type to record the number of minutes, seconds, or fractions of a second[109] since midnight, with a constraint to limit the column to no greater than the number of time units in a day

- **Time of Week**: replace the attribute by two columns, each with the appropriate data type indicated above:
  - one for the day of week, and
  - one for the time of day

- **Day of Week of Month**: replace the attribute by two columns, each with the shortest integer data type available, and each with a constraint to limit the column to the appropriate range of numbers:
  - one for the ordinal (1st, 2nd, 3rd, 4th represented by 1, 2, 3, 4 respectively and 'last' represented by –1 or 5 as appropriate), and
  - one for the day of week

- **Time of Week of Month**: replace the attribute by three columns, each with the appropriate data type as above:
  - two as for **Day of Week of Month**, and
  - one for the time of day

- **Day of Month**: use the shortest integer data type available

- **Day of Year**: use the smallint data type.

---

[108] DB2 and SQL Server provide a time data type for times of day.

[109] The smallint data type is sufficient for minutes, integer allows for milliseconds, while bigint allows for nanoseconds.

11.7.1.6   Columns representing quantifier attributes

There are four main issues to consider with columns representing quantifier attributes:

1. Is this attribute for monetary amounts?
2. Can this attribute legitimately have fractional values?
3. Can this attribute legitimately have negative values?
4. Does the range of allowed values for this attribute vary widely from very large to very small values, e.g., from billions to millionths?

Some DBMSs support a specialized data type[110] for monetary amounts, so all columns holding monetary amounts should use such a data type if available.

Many quantifier attributes (such as counts and ordinals) cannot legitimately have negative or fractional values. Many of these have appeared in various models in this book, e.g., **Order Quantity**, **Unit Price**, **Number of Standing Passengers**, **Emergency Contact Sequence**.

Other quantifier attributes cannot legitimately have negative values but may have fractional values, e.g., **Exchange Rate**, **Blood Alcohol Concentration**.

If the attribute cannot legitimately have fractional values, assign the corresponding column an integer data type or the number data type specified as having no fractional digits.

If the attribute can legitimately have fractional values and some values can only be exactly represented as common fractions (e.g., 1/3), replace the column with a pair of columns with an integer data type, with names ending in **Numerator** and

---

[110] For example in SQL Server there is a money data type.

Denominator. If such values are not required, or do not need to be exact, a single column will suffice: assign the decimal data type, or the number data type specified as having fractional digits. Moreover, if the attribute has a wide range of values, a floating-point data type (e.g., real) allows the decimal point to "float" and thus accommodate both very large and very small values.

Some numeric data types (e.g., tinyint in SQL Server) do not allow negative values, so should not be assigned to a column in which negative values are legitimate.

11.7.1.7 Columns representing media attributes

Unless the DBMS provides specific data types for these, they should be assigned the blob (binary large object) data type.

11.7.2 Internal and external representations

Some data types benefit from using an internal representation that differs from what a user would see. All temporal data types have built-in DBMS support for displaying dates and times in a user-friendly manner while storing them in a non-human friendly form. The only exceptions are (a) days of the week, which require a conversion function to be displayed as day names (Sunday, Monday, etc.), and (b) times of day stored as integers, which require conversion functions to be displayed as hours, minutes, etc.

A further consideration is that if the user base includes both US and non-US users, displayed dates should include month names rather than month numbers. This is because there can be confusion between US format dates and non-US format dates. For example, 7/9/2020 means July 9th 2020 in the US but 7th September elsewhere.

Boolean data benefits from being stored as 0 and 1, but should be displayed as False or True (or No or Yes). Again a conversion function would be required.

In many countries, a multilingual user interface is required. This requires not only that fixed text in web pages be switchable from language to language, but that drop down lists be in the chosen language. For example, a **Travel Class** attribute in an airline booking site might allow the values Business, Premium Economy, and Economy. However, for French-speaking users, these values should be displayed as Classe Affaires, Économique Privilège, and Économique respectively. Achieve this by (a) storing set selection attributes in one language only, with a conversion function to display in other languages as required, or (b) by storing all combinations of Travel Class and Language and filtering by Language when displaying Travel Classes. There may be a similar requirement when there are users in different English-speaking countries. For example, vehicle types are known by different names in the US, the UK, and Australia: a sedan in the US and Australia is a saloon in the UK.

A similar issue arises with Boolean attributes if their values are displayed but, if a Boolean attribute is displayed using a checkbox or pair of radio buttons, only the adjacent text needs to be in the appropriate language, and values in multiple languages don't need to be stored in the database.

11.7.3   Representing composite and multi-valued attributes

Since one of the ways of representing composite and multi-valued attributes in a logical data model involves relationships, discussion of this is deferred to Sections 11.9 and 11.10, which follow the discussion of how to represent relationships.

11.8   Handling relationships

The most common way to represent a 1:n relationship or a 1:1 relationship is with a **foreign key** (as described in Section 11.8.1). Similarly, the most common way to represent an n:n relationship is with an **intersection table** (as described in Section 11.8.4). However, recent versions of many relational DBMSs support **nested tables**, which can be used to represent any kind of relationship, as discussed in Section 11.8.5. Some data modeling tools allow the structure of a nested table to be documented in a logical data model.

11.8.1   1:n relationships

Each 1:n relationship in a business information model can be represented in the corresponding logical data model by including a **foreign key**[111] column in the table representing the entity class at the n end of the relationship. Most (if not all) data modeling tools can do this automatically.

If the relationship is mandatory at the 1 end, all foreign key columns must be mandatory. If the relationship is optional at the 1 end, all foreign key columns must be optional.

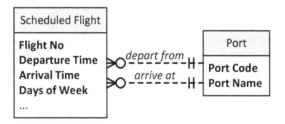

Figure 91: Flight Schedule business information model

---

[111] A **foreign key** is a column (or set of columns) in one table within a relational database referring to either a specific row in another table or another row in the same table.

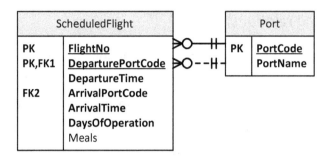

Figure 92: Flight Schedule logical data model (SQL:2003)

There are some things to note about this logical data model:

- It is only suitable for SQL:2003-compliant or object-relational DBMSs, which support the array data type allowing multi-valued attributes to be represented as such. Alternative logical data models that do not rely on the array data type are discussed in Section 11.10.1.

- Two columns (**DeparturePortCode** and **ArrivalPortCode**) have appeared in the **ScheduledFlight** table. These are the foreign keys for each relationship to the **Port** table. It is essential to prefix foreign key column names when there is more than one foreign key to the same table (as in this case). It is also a good idea to prefix foreign key column names when there is only one foreign key to a particular table.

- The primary key of **ScheduledFlight** is not just **FlightNo** but **FlightNo** and **DeparturePortCode** (the columns with underlined names in this particular notation). This is because some Flights are multi-leg—for example, Qantas QF1 flies from Sydney to London Heathrow via Singapore—and each leg needs a separate row in the **ScheduledFlight** table.

- Where a primary key includes a foreign key, the relationship represented by the foreign key is said to be an **identifying relationship**. Only **non-**

transferable[112] relationships should be made into identifying relationships[113].

- Both relationships from **Port** to **ScheduledFlight** are non-transferable[114], but only one foreign key to **Port** is needed in the primary key for uniqueness. Again, *never include more columns in a primary key than are necessary for uniqueness*.

- Identifying relationships are depicted with solid rather than dashed lines in this particular notation. The distinction between solid and dashed lines is different in logical data models from that in business information models:

  o in business information models in this book, solid lines mark relationships to dependent entity classes representing multi-valued attributes or n:n relationships

  o in logical data models in this book, solid lines mark identifying relationships

  o relationships to dependent entity classes in a business information model become identifying relationships in the corresponding logical data model *unless* the enterprise mandates that *all* tables must be given surrogate key

  o some other relationships in a business information model can become identifying relationships in the corresponding logical data model (as in Figure 92).

---

[112] See Section 8.4.6.

[113] As explained in Section 11.6, primary key columns should be invariant.

[114] To avoid customer confusion, a new Flight No is always selected if there is a need for a Flight between different Ports.

11.8.2 1:1 relationships

Like 1:n relationships, these are represented in the corresponding logical data model by adding a foreign key, but only in *one* of the tables involved.

If the relationship is mandatory at one end and optional at the other, add the foreign key column(s), all mandatory, to the table at the optional end of the relationship.

If both ends are mandatory (a rare situation), add the foreign key column(s), all mandatory, to one or the other table.

If both ends are optional, add the foreign key column(s), all optional, to one or the other table.

11.8.3 Overlapping foreign keys

Consider Figure 93, in which foreign keys have been created for each of **VehicleRental**'s relationships (one each with **Vehicle** and **Customer** and two with **Location**). The primary keys of **Vehicle** and **Location** each include a **StateCode** column. Avoid the temptation to create a single **StateCode** column in the **VehicleRental** table. This is because the pick-up and return locations could be in different States, and the Vehicle may have been registered in a third State. Even if there were a restriction that the pick-up and return locations must be in the same State, I would not recommend using a single **StateCode** column in the two foreign keys to **Location**, since that restriction might later be lifted.

As an aside, there appear to be some duplicate columns in the **Vehicle** and **VehicleRental** tables, but those columns serve different purposes. The **CarType**, **Transmission**, **NumberOfSeats**, and **NumberOfDoors** columns in the **VehicleRental** table record the Customer's vehicle selection criteria. By contrast, those columns with the same names in the **Vehicle** table record which criteria each Vehicle meets.

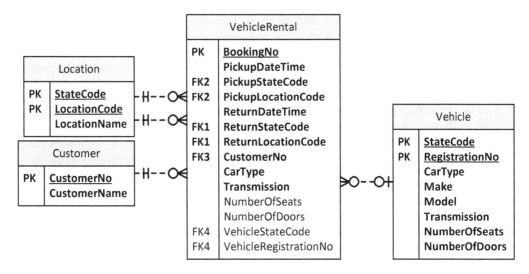

Figure 93: Vehicle Rental logical data model

11.8.4   n:n relationships

Each n:n relationship in a business information model can be represented in the corresponding logical data model by:

1. adding an **intersection table**, with a copy of each of the primary key columns of the tables representing the involved entity classes; these columns (initially at least[115]) become the primary key of the intersection table

2. adding identifying 1:n relationships to the intersection table from each of the tables representing the involved entity classes, which means that each of the primary key columns of the intersection table forms part of the foreign key representing one of the new 1:n relationships

---

[115] As we shall see in Section 11.12.2, the primary key of an intersection table will need to be augmented by a date column if history is to be recorded.

3. if any relationship rules have been documented against the n:n relationship, copying them to a suitable metadata field documenting the intersection table

4. if the n:n relationship has any attributes, adding a column representing each of those attributes to the intersection table

5. deleting the n:n relationship.[116]

This transformation is illustrated in Figure 94 and Figure 95. At least some data modeling tools can perform this transformation automatically.

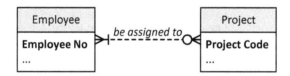

Figure 94: Employee Project Assignments business information model

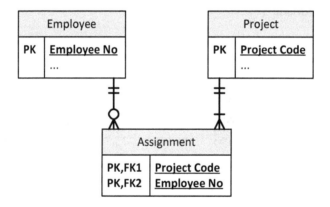

Figure 95: Employee Project Assignments logical data model

Note that, in Figure 94, the relationship between **Project** and **Employee** is mandatory at the **Employee** end. This is not necessarily the case but, in this example, a Project is only set up when at least one Employee has been assigned.

---

[116] We previously encountered this representation of an n:n relationship in Section 5.9.1.

That relationship is optional at the **Project** end because some Employees may be engaged in other than Project work. These cardinalities imply corresponding cardinalities in Figure 95. The mandatory cardinality at the **Employee** end becomes a mandatory cardinality at the n end of the relationship between **Project** and **Assignment**, whereas the optional cardinality at the **Project** end becomes an optional cardinality at the n end of the relationship between **Employee** and **Assignment**.

Note also that, although you might expect to see assignment start and end dates, they weren't included in the business information model and so have not yet been added to the logical data model. Remember, the business information model represents a snapshot *at a point in time*, with data to support history recording (if required) being added to the logical data model later in the process, as described in Section 11.12. If business stakeholders had indicated that assignment start and end dates are important, they would have been added as attributes to the n:n relationship and added to the intersection table as described above.

Intersection tables are examples of **dependent tables**: tables that contain data that cannot exist independently of data in other tables. An Assignment cannot exist without there being an Employee and a Project, whereas Employees and Projects can exist without there being any Assignments.

Many enterprises mandate that each table must be given a surrogate primary key (see Section 11.6.2). Some make an exception for dependent tables. If the enterprise for which you are developing a logical data model mandates surrogate primary keys for *all* tables (including dependent tables), an alternative set of columns is required for the intersection table:

- a single surrogate key column constituting the primary key
- two foreign keys, each replicating the primary key columns of the table representing one of the involved entity classes.

11.8.5   Nested tables

If the target DBMS supports nested tables, this is an alternative way to represent a 1:n relationship but *only* if the entity class at the n end of the relationship has no other relationships. In Figure 96, the **Employee Leave** entity class has no other relationships, so it can be represented by a nested table in a column in the table representing the **Employee** entity class. Some data modeling tools allow the structure of a nested table to be documented in a logical data model.

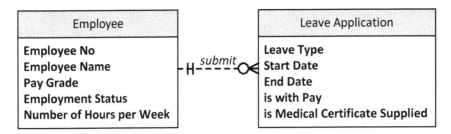

Figure 96: Employee Leave Application business information model

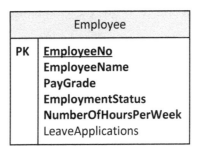

Figure 97: Employee Leave Application logical data model with nested table

An n:n relationship can also be represented as a nested table (in a column in the table representing one of the related entity classes) with foreign key column(s) referencing the table representing the other related entity class.

11.8.6   Hierarchies and acyclic relationship pairs

Before we move on from relationships, we need to add a column to the appropriate table for (a) each recursive relationship representing a hierarchy (see Section 8.4.4.1) and (b) each acyclic relationship pair (see Section 8.4.5.3). This is to allow the relevant rules to be enforced when data is created or updated.

For a hierarchic recursive relationship, I add this column to the table representing the entity class involved in the relationship. For an acyclic relationship pair, I add this column to the table representing the entity class at the 1 end of both relationships in the pair (**Part** in the case of the model in Section 8.4.5.3).

The column to be added should be named **Level**. Its use is explained in Section 11.17.1.4.

11.9   Handling composite attributes

Object-relational DBMSs, SQL:2003-compliant DBMSs, and object-oriented programming environments support composite attributes as such. For example, the SQL:2003 standard includes a row data type[117].

However, in a traditional relational DBMS environment without object-oriented programming, each composite attribute will need to be replaced by multiple columns each representing a component of the attribute.

----

[117] This is referred to as **object** in Oracle.

11.10   Handling multi-valued attributes

11.10.1   Available options

SQL:2003-compliant DBMSs, object-relational DBMSs, and object-oriented programming environments support multi-valued columns as such. For example, the SQL:2003 standard includes an array data type. In such an environment, each multi-valued attribute can be represented by a multi-valued column, as in Figure 92 in Section 11.8.1.

However, in a traditional relational DBMS environment without object-oriented programming, each multi-valued attribute will need to be represented by *one* of the following:

- as many individual columns as the maximum number of values that the attribute can include (only if there is a relatively low upper limit to that number), or

- a **dependent table**, which is an additional table with:

    o   a 1:n relationship from the table representing the original entity class to the new table
    o   one or more columns for the foreign key to the table representing the original entity class
    o   a column to hold an individual value of the original multi-valued attribute
    o   a primary key constraint on the foreign key column(s) plus one other column: either (a) the column holding values of the original multi-valued attribute, or (b) a sequencing column added as described in Section 11.10.2.

For example, the **Days of Operation** and **Meals** attributes in the **Scheduled Flight** entity class in Figure 98 can be represented either as multiple columns (as in Figure 99) or the tables **FlightDay** and **FlightMeal** (as in Figure 100).

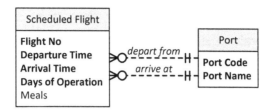

Figure 98: Flight Schedule business information model (revisited)

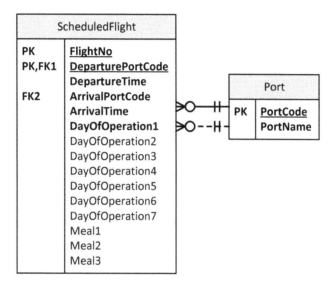

Figure 99: Flight Schedule logical data model (traditional SQL with repeated columns)

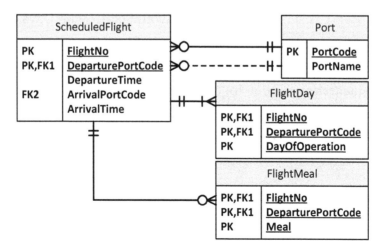

Figure 100: Flight Schedule logical data model (traditional SQL with dependent tables)

Note that, in Figure 100, the primary key of each of the tables created to represent the multi-valued attributes (**FlightDay** and **FlightMeal**) is *all* of the columns.

Note also that, as an alternative to the model in Figure 99, you could replace the seven **DayofOperation*** columns with seven columns representing Boolean attributes (**isOnMonday**, …, **isOnSunday**). If the enterprise mandates that *all* tables must be given a surrogate primary key,

- each of the logical data models depicted above needs an additional column (with a name formed by suffixing the table name with **ID**) to be used as the primary key instead of the column(s) marked as primary keys in the above models
- each set of columns constituting a foreign key must be replaced by a replica of the new primary key of the referenced table.

11.10.2   Multi-valued attribute sequencing

One problem with the model in Figure 100 is that the sequence of Meals in each Flight (which would be preserved in a column with the array data type) might be lost, as Meals would be sequenced alphabetically (Breakfast, Dinner, Lunch, Refreshment, Snack). A similar resequencing would occur with Days of Operation if day names (e.g., Monday) were used instead of integers to represent each day as recommended in Section 11.7.1.5). Meals can be sequenced correctly by (a) adding a **SequenceNo** column to the **FlightMeal** table, and (b) changing the primary key of that table to be **FlightNo**, **DeparturePortCode**, and **SequenceNo** rather than **FlightNo**, **DeparturePortCode**, and **Meal**.

11.11   Handling supertypes and subtypes

SQL:2003-compliant DBMSs and object-oriented programming environments support supertypes and their subtypes. In such an environment, each supertype and its subtypes can be represented by tables in a supertype/subtype relationship, as in Figure 102.

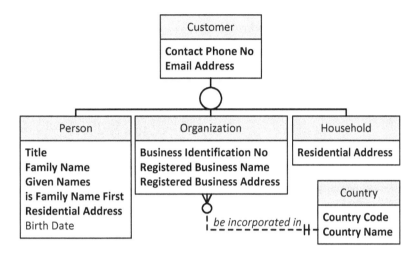

Figure 101: Customer business information model

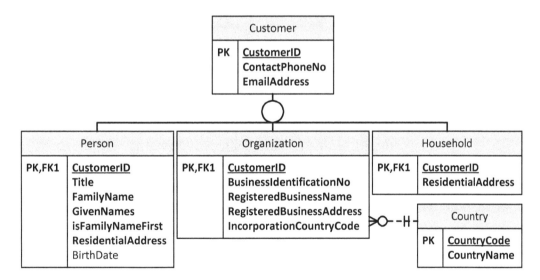

Figure 102: Customer logical data model (SQL:2003)

However, in a traditional relational DBMS environment without object-oriented programming, each supertype and its subtypes must be represented in *one* of the following ways:

1. a table representing the supertype and a table representing each subtype (as in Figure 103), with

    o   all tables with the same primary key
    o   1:1 relationships between the supertype table and each subtype table, mandatory at the supertype table end and optional at the subtype table end
    o   the primary key column(s) in each subtype table acting as the foreign key to the supertype table
    o   all attributes of the supertype represented by columns in the supertype table
    o   all attributes of each subtype represented by columns in the appropriate subtype table

2. a single table representing the supertype (as in Figure 104), with

    o   a column representing each attribute of the supertype
    o   an additional mandatory column in which to record which subtype the row is for
    o   an additional optional column for each attribute of each subtype (but where the same attribute appears in multiple subtypes, only one column), with a conditional mandatory attribute rule (see Section 8.3.1.2) if the attribute is mandatory in the subtype
    o   one or more additional optional columns for each foreign key representing a 1:n relationship to one of the subtypes, with conditional cardinality (see Section 8.4.2) if the opposite end of the relationship to the subtype is mandatory.

I have occasionally encountered a hybrid of these two alternatives, with tables representing the supertype and *some* subtypes. However, the data rules governing such a structure and the allowed processing against it are challenging to design and manage, so I don't recommend this approach.

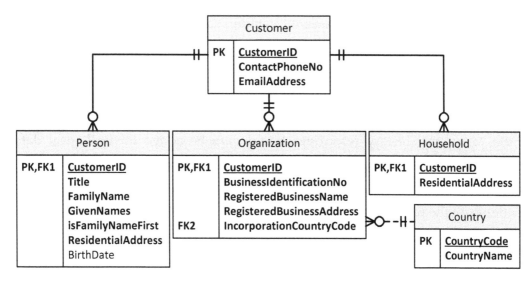

Figure 103: Customer logical data model with supertype table and all subtype tables

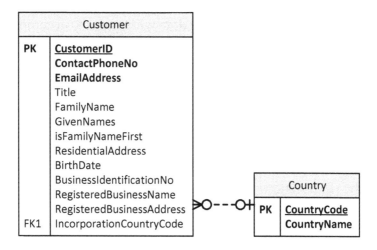

Figure 104: Customer logical data model with supertype table only

A subtype hierarchy may be multi-level (a supertype with subtypes of which at least one has subtypes of its own). Deal with these from the bottom up. For example, in Figure 42 in Section 6.1:

- **Road Vehicle** has subtypes **Powered Vehicle** and **Trailer**

- **Powered Vehicle** has subtypes **Automobile**, **Utility Vehicle**, **Bus**, and **Truck**.

Decide first what to do with **Powered Vehicle** and its subtypes, then what to do with **Road Vehicle** and its subtypes.

11.12   Handling history recording

Data to support history recording should *only* be added to the logical data model if a record of history is required *within* the system being modeled. If the enterprise has a **data warehouse** supporting **business intelligence**, this might better meet the requirement for querying or reporting historical data.

If business stakeholders agree to record history only in the data warehouse:

- no additional data is required in the system being modeled

- the data warehouse model should be reviewed to establish whether any additional data is required in the data warehouse to accommodate new entity classes, attributes, or relationships in the system being modeled (see Section 11.13)

- the system being modeled must be programmed to message the data warehouse whenever a change to data occurs. This can be done via a **trigger** (see Section 11.17.1.1).

If history is to be recorded in the system being modeled, this should be done as described in the next Section.

11.12.1   Recording history in the system being modeled

If the history of changes to one or more variant attributes or transferable 1:n relationships of an entity class is required in the system being modeled:

- add a dependent table named **<table name>Version** (where **<table name>** is the name of the table representing the original entity class), with a primary key consisting of (a) the primary key of the table representing the original entity class (and thus a foreign key), and (b) a column holding the start date of the time period over which the set of variant attribute values applies

- add an optional column holding the end date of the time period over which the set of variant attribute values applies

- move the columns representing each variant attribute and transferable 1:n relationship from the table representing the original entity class to the dependent table.

For example, the logical data model in Figure 105 corresponds exactly to the business information model, whereas in Figure 106:

- the **PersonName**, **ResidentialAddress**, **DeathDate**, and **CitizenshipCountryCode** columns have been moved to the **PersonVersion** table, whereas the **BirthDate** and **BirthCountryCode** columns remain in the **Person** table

- the **CountryName** and **DissolutionDate** columns have been moved to the **CountryVersion** table, whereas the **FormationDate** column remains in the **Country** table.

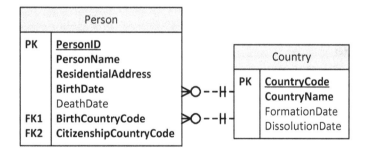

Figure 105: Personal details logical data model (history not required)

Creation of versions needs to occur automatically when any time-variant attribute or transferable relationship is updated, as discussed in Section 11.17.2.

These models assume that a Person cannot have dual citizenship at any time. Section 11.12.2 depicts a model that allows dual citizenship.

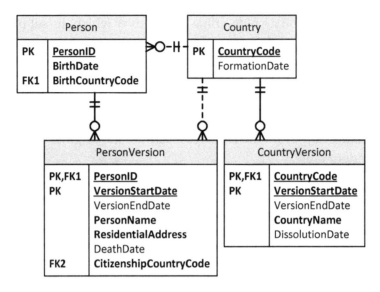

Figure 106: Personal details logical data model (history required)

11.12.2   n:n relationships

If the history of an n:n relationship (modeled using an intersection table) is required,

- add **StartDate** and **EndDate** columns to the intersection table
- add the **StartDate** column to the primary key of the intersection table.

Applying this to the Citizenship relationship, we get the model in Figure 107.

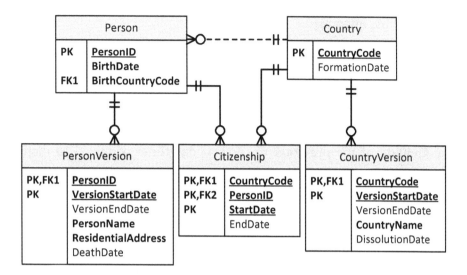

Figure 107: Personal details logical data model (dual citizenship)

11.12.3   Versioning granularity

It is important to establish whether each version of a table or relationship is deemed to change at midnight or can change at different times of day. Changing at midnight requires only start and end dates in the Version table, and establishing which Version was effective on a given date involves the between operator[118]. All of the examples provided so far in assume this situation.

If versions can change at different times of day, start and end *datetimes* are required in the Version table rather than dates, and the predicate DateTime >= StartDateTime and Date < EndDateTime must be used to establish which Version was effective at a given time on a given date[119].

---

[118] Use the predicate Date between StartDate and EndDate.

[119] The predicate DateTime between StartDateTime and EndDateTime is equivalent to DateTime >= StartDateTime and Date <= EndDateTime.

11.12.4   Versioning integrity

It is important to ensure that when a date or datetime is supplied, exactly one Version is returned for each variant entity instance. This requires that there be no overlap and no gaps between Versions. If dates rather than datetimes are used to distinguish Versions, the **StartDate** of each Version must be one day later than the **EndDate** of the previous Version. If datetimes are used to distinguish Versions, the **StartDateTime** of each Version must equal the **EndDateTime** of the previous Version.

The following are also required in most circumstances:

- the **StartDate** or **StartDateTime** of the earliest Version must be no earlier than the **StartDate** (or equivalent) of the entity instance itself (e.g., the **StartDate** of an Employee, the **RegistrationDate** of an Organization, the **BirthDate** of a Person)
- the **EndDate** or **EndDateTime** of the latest Version must be no later than the **EndDate** (or equivalent) of the entity instance itself.

These requirements can be managed as described in Section 11.17.2.

11.12.5   6th Normal Form

The previous sections recommend you add a single dependent table to hold *all* variant attributes of an entity class. However, this can lead to redundancy where one or more attributes change significantly more slowly than others. For example, if a Person changes their Country of Citizenship a few times but never changes their Name, each row of the **PersonVersion** table for that Person will have the same value in the **Name** column.

To avoid this redundancy, (Date, Darwen, & Lorentzos, 2003) proposes that a separate dependent table be added for each variant attribute. In this case, the

PersonVersion table would be replaced by three tables, each with a primary key consisting of columns **PersonID** and **VersionStartDate**:

- a **PersonNameVersion** table, with non-key **PersonName** and **VersionEndDate** columns

- a **PersonAddressVersion** table, with non-key **ResidentialAddress** and **VersionEndDate** columns

- a **PersonCitizenshipVersion** table, with non-key **CitizenshipCountryID** and **VersionEndDate** columns.

Unlike the structure illustrated in Figure 106, this structure would be in 6th Normal Form. **Death Date** should be moved to **Person**.

11.13   Data warehousing

Data warehousing is the extraction of data from operational systems into an integrated data repository (a **data warehouse**). **Business intelligence** involves analysis of historical and current data in the warehouse to inform business decision-making.

There are two schools of thought about achieving this:

- Ralph Kimball favors a data warehouse consisting only of unnormalized **dimensional models** populated directly from operational databases.[120]

---

[120] Kimball is correct to say that a dimensional model is better than a normalized enterprise-wide data warehouse model for intuitive access by end-users. However, he states incorrectly (in his 1997 Dimensional Modeling Manifesto) *"End users cannot understand, remember [or] navigate an ER model. There is no graphical user interface that takes a general ER model and makes it usable by end users. Software cannot usefully query a general ER model."* These statements may be true of a normalized enterprise-wide data warehouse, but ER (Entity-Relationship) is a modeling technique, used in Figure 109 to represent a dimensional model, which disproves Kimball's assertions.

- Bill Inmon favors a normalized data warehouse populated from operational databases from which data is extracted into **data marts**, each with a dimensional model (see Section 11.13.2).

I recommend the Inmon approach, with a data warehouse business information model formed by (a) merging the business information models of its source systems, and (b) adding the time dimension.

11.13.1   Data vault

The ideal logical data model for the Inmon data warehouse is one structured as a **data vault**, as developed by Dan Linstedt in 2000. Its principal advantage, in my view, is that any additional data requirements can be added to the model without any existing data structures needing to be changed. It achieves this by treating all attributes as potentially variable, and all relationships as potentially n:n.

A data vault logical data model consists of three types of table:

- **Hubs** corresponding to business information model entity classes
- **Satellites** holding time-variant Hub attributes
- **Links** corresponding to business information model relationships.

The model in Figure 108 is the data vault equivalent of the model in Figure 107.

Note:

- The naming standard for data vault schemas is to suffix each table name with **_Hub**, **_Sat**, or **_Link** according to the table type.
- Each table has **_HashKey**, **LoadDateTime**, and **RecordSource** columns.
- The **LoadDateTime** column records when new data about the Person, Country, or Citizenship was *loaded*, not when the change occurred in the real world (which is recorded in **StartDate**). This allows not only questions like "what was this Person's Name on date x" but questions

like "what was our knowledge of this Person's Name on date *x*" to be answered. Data models that support both question types are referred to as **bi-temporal** models.

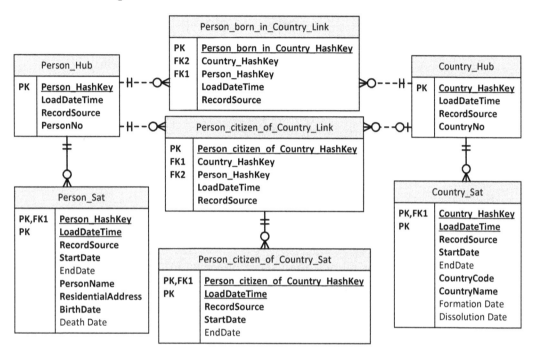

Figure 108: Data vault logical data model

11.13.2 Dimensional models

A **dimensional model** is a specific data structure recommended where end-user analytic queries are to be supported. It consists of a number of **star schemas**, each with a central **fact** entity class related to multiple **dimension** entity classes. For example, Figure 109 models a record of supermarket purchases by loyalty program customers.

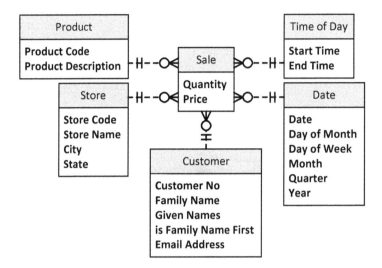

Figure 109: Star schema[121]

This model is unnormalized, as there is obvious redundancy, particularly in the **Date** entity class, but this allows analysis of purchasing trends at different times of the week or month. The **Time of Day** entity class can be used to divide the day into a set of time ranges, e.g., before 9am, 9am-midday, midday-5pm, 5pm-7pm, after 7pm.

The dimension entity classes can be shared by multiple star schemas.

11.14   Handling data rules

Most data rules documented in the business information model can be transferred as such to the logical data model. However, some will need adjustment. Furthermore, some additional data rules will be required in the logical data model.

---

[121] The fact table is named **Sale** rather than **Purchase** as the events recorded are Sales from the enterprise's point of view.

11.14.1 Rules inherited from the business information model

11.14.1.1 Attribute rules

Each attribute rule governing a particular attribute becomes a rule governing the corresponding column—no rewording is required. If the attribute rules have been documented in the data modeling tool, the process of copying the business information model to the logical data model (described in Section 11.2) should automatically copy any attribute rule to the logical data model. If the attribute rules have been documented as rule statements in a separate document, that document can continue to serve as the source of attribute rules for the logical data model.

11.14.1.2 Relationship rules

Each column created as part of a foreign key is mandatory or optional as defined in Section 11.8.1.

If any other relationship rules governing a 1:n or 1:1 relationship have been documented in the data modeling tool, the process of copying the business information model to the logical data model should also automatically copy those rules to the logical data model. If they have instead been documented as rule statements in a separate document, that document can continue to serve as the source of other relationship rules for the logical data model.

11.14.1.3 Uniqueness rules

Section 8.6.3 recommends that uniqueness rules be documented as rule statements in a separate document. That document can continue to serve as the source of uniqueness rules for the logical data model.

11.14.2 Additional rules

Additional rules are required for primary and foreign keys, and supertypes and their subtypes.

Primary key and foreign key rules are an automatic consequence of defining columns as primary key or foreign key columns (see Sections 11.6 and 11.8.1).

Supertype/subtype rules need to be added manually. The rules required vary according to how the supertype/subtype set has been represented (see Section 11.11):

- as a set of tables in an explicit supertype/subtype relationship in an object-relational DBMS or SQL:2003-compliant DBMS
- as a table representing the supertype and a table representing each subtype, or
- as a single table representing the supertype.

If it has been represented as an explicit supertype/subtype relationship, no additional rules are required.

If it has been represented as a table representing the supertype and a table representing each subtype, the only additional rules required are as follows:

- If the subtypes are mutually exclusive (see Section 6.2), for each row in the supertype table, there must be a maximum of one row in one of the subtype tables.
- If the subtypes are jointly exhaustive (see Section 6.3), for each row in the supertype table, there must be a minimum of one row in one of the subtype tables.

If it has been represented as a single table representing the supertype, an additional conditional mandatory attribute rule (see Section 8.3.1.2) is required for each mandatory attribute in each subtype, along the lines of

> Each **Road Vehicle** in which **Vehicle Type** is Bus must specify exactly one **Number of Standing Passengers**.

11.15   Supporting programming, improving performance

There are some additions which can be made to the logical data model in some situations to support the programming task and improve the performance of data retrieval processes.

11.15.1   Views

Data update and retrieval processes use **database queries** to access tables. These queries select rows and columns from one or more tables. A query that accesses multiple tables does so either by:

- a **join**: matching values in related columns (typically primary and foreign keys), or by
- a **union** in which some rows come from one table, and other rows come from one or more other tables.

Queries may include **subqueries**, which return results to be used as a virtual table in the containing query.

Developers often find that they use the same subquery in multiple queries or code the same query in multiple processes. A **view** is a virtual table containing the result of a database query, and can be created once then referred to (as if it were a table) in multiple queries or processes.

Developers should advise the data modeler of this situation when it arises, and the data modeler should collaborate with the developers to design views to meet their needs. The data modeler should then add these to the logical data model, which continues to be the repository of *all* data resources in the database.

11.15.2   Denormalization

Denormalization is a technique that was employed in the early days of relational databases to improve performance. It involves the replication of columns from other tables to avoid queries having to include joins with those other tables, and/or storage of calculated data to avoid the need for calculation "on the fly".

Denormalization reintroduces the problem of **update anomalies** discussed in Section 4.2, and so *should be avoided*. Other ways to improve performance without resorting to denormalization include:

- **indexes** (see Section 11.17.3.1)
- **materialized views**, which are views which are stored in the database under DBMS control rather than being populated "on the fly".

If denormalization *is* employed:

- each added column should be recorded in the logical data model with an annotation indicating the source of the data
- process designers and programmers must be advised of the need to
    - update any added column whenever the source data is updated
    - prevent independent update of any added column.

11.16   Replicating business information model changes

If the business information model changes after the corresponding logical data model is created, all business information model changes must be replicated in the logical data model:

- If an entity class is added

    o copy it and its attributes to the logical data model
    o rename the resulting table and columns as described in Sections 11.4 and 11.5
    o add a primary key, as described in Section 11.6
    o handle each column as described in Section 11.7.

- If an attribute is added to an existing entity

    o copy it to the logical data model
    o rename the resulting column as described in Section 11.5
    o handle the column as described in Section 11.7.

- If a relationship is added

    o copy it to the logical data model
    o handle it as described in Section 11.8.

- If an entity class is removed, remove the corresponding table from the logical data model.

- If an attribute is removed, remove the corresponding column from the logical data model.

- If a relationship is removed

    o if it is a 1:n relationship represented in the logical data model using a foreign key, remove the corresponding relationship from the logical data model, which should automatically remove the foreign key column (if any)
    o if it is an n:n relationship represented in the logical data model using an intersection table, remove that table
    o if it has been represented in the logical data model using an array data type, remove the array column.

- If the data type of an attribute is changed, change the DBMS data type of the corresponding column as described in Section 11.7.1.

- If an attribute or relationship not previously requiring history now requires it, handle it as described in Section 11.12.

- If an attribute or relationship previously requiring history no longer requires it

  - o   if history is being recorded *within* the system being modeled, remove the additional data that was added for recording history as described in Section 11.12
  - o   if history is being recorded in a data warehouse, advise the developers that a message to the data warehouse is no longer required whenever a change to the attribute or relationship occurs.

11.17   Implementing in a relational DBMS

All data modeling tools I have encountered automatically generate **DDL** (**Data Definition Language**) scripts from a logical data model, suitable for input to a specific relational DBMS[122]. When input to the DBMS, the DDL script creates each table, with its columns (with specified data type and marked as mandatory[123] or not) and primary and foreign key constraints.

11.17.1   Managing other data rules

Those data modeling tools that support uniqueness rules other than on the primary key should also include the corresponding uniqueness constraints in the DDL script.

All other data rules (including uniqueness rules not supported by the data modeling tool) have to be added manually.

---

[122] Different DBMSs have slightly different DDL syntax and data types.
[123] Mandatory attributes are marked using the NOT NULL clause in DDL.

11.17.1.1 Documented data rules

Simple data rules can be implemented using DDL **constraints**. Apart from NOT NULL, PRIMARY KEY, and FOREIGN KEY constraints (created automatically), there are:

- UNIQUE constraints (which enforce uniqueness rules), and
- CHECK constraints (which enforce some other rules).

An example of a UNIQUE constraint is:

- CONSTRAINT OrderItemU1 UNIQUE (OrderNo, ProductCode).

Some examples of CHECK constraints are:

- CONSTRAINT FlightBookingRequestC1 CHECK
  (TravelClass IN ('First','Business','Premium Economy','Economy'))
- CONSTRAINT FlightBookingRequestC2 CHECK
  (PassengerCount BETWEEN 1 AND 9)
- CONSTRAINT LeaveRequestC1 CHECK
  (EndDate >= StartDate)
- CONSTRAINT ScheduledFlightC1 CHECK
  (ArrivalPortCode != DeparturePortCode).

Other rules have to be implemented in code, either in process code or in a **trigger**. This is a piece of code that runs automatically when a defined action (typically an insert, update, or delete of data in a database table) occurs.

The data modeler, therefore, needs to provide both the database administrator and developers with:

- a list of all data rules
- each occurrence of any of the situations described in Sections 11.17.1.2, 11.17.1.3, and 11.17.1.4, each of which
  - requires specific database updates to occur, and
  - requires that other updates be prevented.

11.17.1.2 Relationships that are mandatory at the n end

If a relationship is mandatory at the n end:

- whenever a row is inserted in the table at the 1 end, at least one row must be inserted in the table at the n end before the **transaction** is **committed**[124]

- whenever an attempt is made to delete from the table at the n end the last remaining row associated with a row in the table at the 1 end, that deletion must be prevented.

11.17.1.3 Supertypes and subtypes

The rules governing these are listed in Section 11.14.2.

11.17.1.4 Hierarchies and acyclic relationship pairs

In Sections 8.4.4.1 and 8.4.4.3, we established that recursive relationships representing hierarchies are acyclic and irreflexive. In Section 8.4.5.3, we encountered an acyclic relationship pair.

In Section 11.8.6, I recommended that, in each of these situations, a column named **Level** be added to the table representing the appropriate entity class.

This column should be automatically populated whenever a row is inserted in the table:

- If no higher-level instance is identified at insertion time (e.g., an Employee row is inserted without a Manager being identified), **Level** should be set to zero.

- If a higher-level instance is identified at insertion time, **Level** should be set to one less than the **Level** of that higher-level instance.

---

[124] See Section 11.17.4.

If a higher-level instance is identified during a later update:

- if **Level** is currently zero, **Level** should be set to one less than the **Level** of that higher-level instance

- if **Level** is not currently zero:

  - if the **Level** of that higher-level instance is currently zero, the **Level** of that higher-level instance should be set to one more than **Level** in the row being inserted or updated
  - if the **Level** of that higher-level instance is not currently zero and is less than **Level** in the row being inserted or updated, the insertion or update should be rejected.

11.17.2   Updating data

If the history of changes to one or more variant attributes or transferable 1:n relationships is to be recorded only in the data warehouse (see Section 11.12), the system must be programmed to message the data warehouse whenever a change to data occurs. This can be done via a **trigger** (see Section 11.17.1.1).

By contrast, if change history is to be recorded in the operational system database:

- whenever a row is inserted in the table representing that entity class, another row must be inserted in the corresponding version table, in which **EndDate** is null[125], and **StartDate** records the date when the entity instance in question is deemed to have started in the real world (e.g., Registration Date, Birth Date), *not* the date when the row is inserted

---

[125] An alternative to null that is favored by some developers is some arbitrary far future date such as 31st December 9999.

- whenever one or more of the columns representing variant attributes or transferable 1:n relationships is updated:
  - another row must be inserted in the corresponding version table, in which **EndDate** is null, and **StartDate** records the date when the attributes or relationships in question are deemed to have changed in the real world (e.g., Registration Date, Birth Date), *not* the date when the row is updated
  - **EndDate** in the previously latest row in the version table representing the same entity instance must be updated to the same value as **StartDate** in the version row just inserted
- whenever an attempt is made to delete from the table representing that entity class:
  - that deletion must be prevented
  - **EndDate** in the latest row in the version table representing the same entity instance must be updated to the date when the entity instance in question is deemed to have finished in the real world (e.g., Dissolution Date, Death Date), *not* the date of the delete attempt.

If a new instance of an n:n relationship is required, **StartDate** in the inserted row must record when the relationship instance in question is deemed to have started in the real world (e.g., Assignment Date), *not* the date when the row is inserted. If an attempt is made to delete an instance of an n:n relationship:

- that deletion must be prevented
- **EndDate** in the inserted row must record when the relationship instance in question is deemed to have finished in the real world (e.g., Assignment End Date), *not* the date of the delete attempt.

If versions can change at different times of day, replace **StartDate** and **EndDate** in the above logic with **StartDateTime** and **EndDateTime**.

11.17.3   Improving performance

SQL is non-procedural: the developer can only specify what data is required, not how to obtain it from the database. The DBMS's **optimizer** determines the optimum method for obtaining the results of each query, which it documents in a **Query Execution Plan**. The following sections provide a high-level overview of some of the performance improvement measures available in a relational DBMS. Any of them can be added to the physical database (and subsequently adjusted) without changing the **logical schema** (the tables and columns as specified in the logical data model) and hence without requiring any change to program code already written.

11.17.3.1 Indexes

Most (if not all) relational DBMSs manage primary keys and uniqueness constraints using **unique indexes**[126]—created and maintained automatically by the DBMS—on the relevant columns.

Additional indexes, both unique and **non-unique**[127], can be created by a database administrator. If carefully chosen, they can improve query performance, although inserts, updates, and deletes against a table may be slower with more indexes. In particular, non-unique indexes on column(s) which have the same value(s) in many rows can take a significant time to update in connection with an insert, update, or delete operation.

---

[126] A unique index is one which does not allow duplicate values in the indexed column(s), e.g., an index on the Employee No column in an **Employee** table (each Employee must have a different Employee No).

[127] A non-unique index is one which allows duplicate values in the indexed column(s), e.g., an index on the **Pay Grade** column in an **Employee** table (more than one Employee can have the same Pay Grade).

An index may be **clustered** or **non-clustered**. A clustered index sorts the data in the table using the indexed columns whereas a non-clustered index is a separate sorted dataset (like the index of a book).

If a query only returns columns that are in one or more indexes, the table(s) themselves do not have to be accessed.

Among the most useful additional indexes are those on foreign key columns and on columns that are often referenced in queries.

Even if an index is created to improve the performance of a particular query, there is no guarantee that the optimizer will use it. To establish what indexes a query uses, a developer or database administrator can run the query then check the Query Execution Plan created by the DBMS[128]. If the query doesn't use the index, one or more of the following may work:

- rewrite the query in a different but logically-equivalent form
- modify the index by adding or removing columns
- select a different index on the underlying table to use as the **clustering index**.

11.17.3.2 Other performance improvement measures

Various physical table properties can be specified by a database administrator to improve query performance. These include:

- using a dedicated database server rather than a shared server
- providing it with sufficient resources, such as processor(s), memory, and disk drives

---

[128] A Query Execution Plan may not be automatically generated. The user may need to specify in advance whether a Query Execution Plan is to be generated.

- placing certain tables in different tablespaces and/or on different disk drives

- using a different disk drive for the log files used for recovery (see Section 11.17.4).

The performance of inserts, updates, deletes, and queries against a table to which significant amounts of data are being added can be improved by setting the **fill factors**[129] for a table and its indexes to a value less than 100%. Doing this allows new rows to be inserted into the database pages (data blocks) where data access routines would expect to find them, rather than in **overflow pages**[130]. As more rows are inserted into overflow pages, operations against the table are slowed down. The DBMS should be tasked with **reorganizing**[131] each such table regularly.

11.17.4 Managing security

It is outside the scope of this book to cover security in any detail. However, a data modeler should be aware of the security facilities available to the database administrator in the target DBMS.

Most (if not all) DBMSs provide the following security facilities:

----

[129] The **fill factor** of a table or index determines the percentage of space on each leaf-level page (data block) to be filled with data or index entries, reserving the remainder on each page as free space for future growth.

[130] An **overflow page** is a page (data block) in which rows are placed when there is no room for them in the page where data access routines would expect to find them.

[131] **Reorganizing** a table or index is the process of sorting all rows or index entries and distributing them across the pages (data blocks) according to the fill factor, so that data access routines can correctly predict where to find them.

- creation of **user groups** (corresponding to job roles) to which specific access permissions can be granted, allowing users assigned to those groups to update specific data, or only to read specific data

- **commit** and **rollback** facilities, to ensure that a **transaction** (set of database updates) is either executed to completion (committed) or canceled (rolled back) to ensure that the database is always left in a consistent state

- **mirroring**: the management of multiple copies of a database to support database restoration after failure, enhance database availability, and optimize performance.

11.18   Summary

Once the business information model has been accepted by business stakeholders, developers need a logical data model against which to write code (unless the target data platform is XML).

A logical data model can be developed from the business information model by a series of well-defined steps, including:

1. removing derived data items
2. renaming tables and columns to conform to the naming standard in force
3. adding primary keys
4. handling columns
5. handling relationships
6. handling composite and multi-valued attributes
7. handling supertypes and subtypes
8. handling history recording
9. handling data rules.

The data modeler should collaborate with the developers to design views to meet their needs, and then add these to the logical data model.

Denormalization should be avoided as it reintroduces the problem of update anomalies.

If the business information model changes after the corresponding logical data model is created, all business information model changes must be replicated in the logical data model.

Data modeling tools can generate DDL scripts from the logical data model, for input to the DBMS to create each table, column, and primary and foreign key constraint. Other data rules have to be added manually.

Various performance improvement measures can be applied to the database without changing the table structure, and hence without requiring any change to program code.

Chapter 12.   Modeling XML data

XML (**Extensible Markup Language**) is used for various purposes, of which arguably the most common are messaging between systems and publication of data for consumption by other systems.

One example of its use for messaging between systems is in electronic conveyancing, where real estate transactions can be executed electronically through:

- electronic preparation of documentation
- electronic verification of documentation against land title legislation and associated business rules
- electronic recording and management of settlement (exchange of contracts and money)
- electronic lodgment of documentation with the appropriate Land Registry.

One example of its use for publication of data for consumption by other systems is the use of XML by rail network asset management authorities to publish data describing the rail network, for use by timetabling, operations, train control, signaling, and engineering systems.

12.1   XML data structures

Whatever the target data platform, a data modeler needs to understand both business information requirements and the data structures available in that data platform. Let us therefore look at some example XML data that might support the two applications referred to above.

Figure 110 depicts a small fragment[132] of XML data that could be used to describe a rail network.

```xml
<?xml version="1.0" encoding="UTF-8"?>
<Geography Version="5.12" Date="2020-10-25">
  <Nodes>
    <Node Code="LDFC" Name="Lindfield South Turnback" PlatformNo="" IsTimingPoint="false"
        IsJunction="true" IsBufferStop="false" SchematicX="496" SchematicY="626">
      <TurnBans>
        <TurnBan FromNode="LDFA" ToNode="LDFB"/>
      </TurnBans>
    </Node>
    <Node Code="LDFB" Name="Lindfield South from Turnback" PlatformNo="" IsTimingPoint="false"
        IsJunction="true" IsBufferStop="false" SchematicX="496" SchematicY="628"/>
    <Node Code="LDFA" Name="Lindfield South to Turnback" PlatformNo="" IsTimingPoint="false"
        IsJunction="true" IsBufferStop="false" SchematicX="494" SchematicY="628"/>
  </Nodes>
  <Links>
    <Link FromNode="LDFA" ToNode="LDFC" IsSiding="false" IsCrossover="true"
        IsRunningLine="false" TrackCode="" Electrification="1500vDC" Length="75"/>
    <Link FromNode="LDFC" ToNode="LDFB" IsSiding="false" IsCrossover="true"
        IsRunningLine="false" TrackCode="" Electrification="1500vDC" Length="75"/>
  </Links>
</Geography>
```

Figure 110: Rail network XML data example

XML data is composed of **elements**, each of which may contain other elements, in this case a single **Geography** element, containing:

- a single **Nodes** element, containing multiple **Node** elements, each of which may contain an optional single **TurnBans** element, containing one or more **TurnBan** elements

- a single **Links** element, containing multiple **Link** elements.

---

[132] There would be many thousands of Nodes and Links in reality.

Each element:

- starts with a **start tag**, consisting of the '<' character followed by the element name followed in turn by the '>' character if the element contains other elements

- ends with an **end tag**:
  - the characters '/>', if the element contains no other elements
  - the characters '</' followed by the element name and the '>' character, if the element contains other elements

- may contain **XML attributes**[133], each of which is a name-value pair (e.g., **FromNode** = 'LDFA', **ToNode** = 'LDFC'), in which the value is a string which may be empty (e.g., **TrackCode** = '').

Note that the values of the **FromNode** and **ToNode** attributes of **Links** are references to **Code** attributes of **Nodes**.

To establish whether a proposed XML data structure fulfils requirements, it should be depicted as a business information model. This can be done by following three simple rules:

1. Any plural element that contains *only* one or more corresponding singular element (**Nodes**, **Turn Bans**, **Links** in Figure 111) is not explicitly modeled but implied by a 1:n relationship line.

2. Each non-plural element that contains other elements is modeled as an entity class box (**Geography**, **Node**, **Turn Ban**, **Link** in Figure 111) with a *solid* 1:n or 1:1 relationship line to each of the other elements it contains.

3. Each XML attribute is modeled as either:
   - an attribute within an entity class box if it *is not* a reference to another element (e.g., **Name**), or

---

[133] These are referred to simply as **attributes** in discussion of XML data, but I use the term **XML attribute** to avoid confusion with attributes in a data model.

o   a *dashed* relationship line if it *is* a reference to another element (e.g., *be from*).

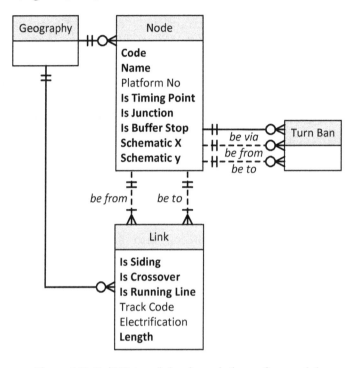

Figure 111: Rail Network business information model

Figure 112 depicts a fictional example of XML data typically provided when initiating a real estate mortgage. This data conforms to a **schema** that:

- uses subordinate elements rather than XML attributes, and

- uses **empty-element tags** (e.g., **<DocumentReference/>**), to represent optional elements that are not supplied (rather than completely omitting the element, e.g., **TurnBans** in Figure 110).

```
<?xml version="1.0"?>
<MortgageForm>
    <DocumentReference/>
    <Jurisdiction>NSW</Jurisdiction>
    <LandTitles>
        <LandTitle>DP56789</LandTitle>
    </LandTitles>
    <Mortgagees>
        <Mortgagee>
            <CompanyNo>123456789</CompanyNo>
            <MortgageeSignatory>
                <ExecuteSealType>AUTHOFF</ExecuteSealType>
                <SignType>USINGSEAL</SignType>
                <SignerCount>1</SignerCount>
                <Signers>
                    <Signer>
                        <SignerName>JOE BLOW</SignerName>
                        <SignerRole>AUTHORISED OFFICER</SignerRole>
                    </Signer>
                </Signers>
            </MortgageeSignatory>
            <MortgageeType>COR</MortgageeType>
            <OrganisationName>BANK OF BOURKE</OrganisationName>
        </Mortgagee>
    </Mortgagees>
    <Mortgagors>
        <Mortgagor>
            <FamilyName>SMITH</FamilyName>
            <GivenName>JOHN</GivenName>
            <MortgagorSignatory>
                <SignType>SELF</SignType>
            </MortgagorSignatory>
        </Mortgagor>
    </Mortgagors>
</MortgageForm>
```

Figure 112: Conveyancing XML data example

This data is composed of a single **MortgageForm** element, containing:

- single **DocumentReference** and **Jurisdiction** elements

- a single **LandTitles** element, containing one or more **LandTitle** elements

- a single **Mortgagees** element, containing one or more **Mortgagee** elements, each of which contains:

  o a single **CompanyNo** element

- o a **MortgageeSignatory** element, containing four sub-elements, one of which (**Signers**) contains one or more **Signer** elements, each containing **SignerName** and **SignerRole** elements
- o single **MortgageeType** and **OrganisationName**[134] elements
- a single **Mortgagors** element, containing one or more **Mortgagor** elements, each of which contains:
  - o single **FamilyName** and **GivenName** elements
  - o a **MortgagorSignatory** element, which contains a **SignType** element (and would contain other elements if **SignType** were other than "SELF").

To produce a complete model of this data, we would need to establish what other data is included in alternative situations. For example, if a Mortgagor were a company rather than an individual, the relevant **Mortgagor** element would contain the same subordinate elements as a **Mortgagee** element, albeit with different values. You can use whatever symbol your data modeling tool uses to indicate subtypes to enable the alternative subordinate elements to be shown. If the tool allows entity class names to be parenthesized, this should be done for each alternative, as these names will not appear in the XML schema.

Earlier in this section I stated three rules for depicting an XML data structure as a business information model. An additional rule is required if subordinate elements are to be used rather than XML attributes:

4. Each subordinate element that does not contain other subordinate elements should be modeled as an attribute within an entity box.

This is illustrated in Figure 113.

---

[134] This is the UK/Australian spelling.

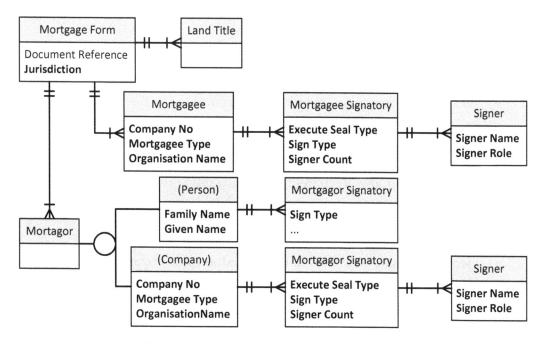

Figure 113: Mortgage business information model

Note that the Mortgagee must be a company, whereas a Mortgagor can be an individual or a company, for which different data is required.

12.2   XML schemas

Once the business information model is approved, it is a simple matter to derive the structure of the required XML dataset, and document it as an **XML schema**, often referred to as an **XSD**. These are used to document the subordinate elements (if any) within each element, each with:

- a data type, one of:
  - a primitive data type (these generally correlate to those provided by DBMSs)
  - a derived data type pre-defined in the XSD specification in terms of one or more of the primitive data types

o a derived data type defined by the user creating the specific schema

- the minimum and maximum number allowed

- whether the element is an alternative to another (such as Company data as an alternative to Person data in the mortgage data in Figure 112)

- the XML attributes (if any) of the element.

An XML schema can also document the constraints on the values allowed in each user-created derived data type, such as those illustrated in Figure 114, which restrict:

- elements assigned the **Class** data type to the values Economy, Premium Economy, Business, and First, and

- elements assigned the **City** data type to 3 letters.

```xml
<xs:simpleType name="ClassDT">
    <xs:restriction base="xs:string">
        <xs:enumeration value="Economy"/>
        <xs:enumeration
            value="Premium Economy"/>
        <xs:enumeration value="Business"/>
        <xs:enumeration value="First"/>
    </xs:restriction>
</xs:simpleType>

<xs:simpleType name="CityDT">
    <xs:restriction base="xs:string">
        <xs:minLength value="3"/>
        <xs:maxLength value="3"/>
        <xs:pattern value="([A-Z])*" />
    </xs:restriction>
</xs:simpleType>
```

Figure 114: XML data type constraints

In a business information model intended for implementation in XML, you should use attribute classes[135] rather than the XML data types, then map each attribute class to the appropriate XML data type.

---

[135] See Section 4.7.

Note that a business information model (as defined in Part 1) provides all the information needed to define the elements in the XML schema, except:

- whether to use subordinate elements or XML attributes
- whether to use empty-element tags or completely omit optional elements without values.

For this reason, it is not necessary to create a logical data model. Moreover, a logical data model is not suitable as a representation of an XML schema since the latter do not use foreign keys.

12.3   Summary

XML represents data as a hierarchy of elements, any of which may include XML attributes.

To establish whether a proposed XML data structure fulfils requirements, it should be depicted as a business information model, by following some simple rules.

Once the business information model is approved, it is a simple matter to derive the structure of the required XML dataset. An XML schema can then be used to define that structure and constraints on data therein.

Suggested Reading

Date, C. J., Darwen, H., & Lorentzos, N. A. (2003). *Temporal Data and the Relational Model.* Morgan Kaufman.

Giles, J. (2019). *The Elephant in the Fridge: Guided Steps to Data Vault Success through Building Business-Centered Models.* Technics Publications.

Halpin, T. (2015). *Object-Role Modeling Fundamentals: A Practical Guide to Data Modeling with ORM.* Technics Publications.

Hay, D. (2003). *Requirements Analysis: From Business Views to Architecture.* Prentice Hall PTR.

Hoberman, S. (2005). *Data Modeling Made Simple.* Technics Publications.

Kent, W. (2015). *Data and Reality.* Technics Publications.

Object Management Group. (2019, Dec). *Semantics of Business Vocabulary and Business Rules.*

Pascal, F. (2000). *Practical Issues in Database Management: A Reference for the Thinking Practitioner.* Addison-Wesley.

Simsion, G. C., & Witt, G. C. (2004). *Data Modeling Essentials* (3rd ed.). Morgan Kaufmann.

Stonebraker, M., & Moore, D. (1996). *Object-Relational DBMSs: The Next Great Wave.* Morgan Kaufmann.

Witt, G. C. (2012). *Writing Effective Business Rules: A Practical Method.* Morgan Kaufmann.

Index

www.ingramcontent.com/pod-product-compliance
Lightning Source LLC
Chambersburg PA
CBHW080627060326
40690CB00021B/4843